FINDING WOUNDED DEER

FINDING WOUNDED DEER

A Comprehensive Guide to Tracking Deer Shot with Bow or Gun

John Trout, Jr.

Foreword by Peter J. Fiduccia

Skyhorse Publishing

Skyhorse Publishing books may be purchased in bulk at special discounts for sales promotion, corporate gifts, fund-raising, or educational purposes. Special editions can also be created to specifications. For details, contact the Special Sales Department, Skyhorse Publishing, 307 West 36th Street, 11th Floor, New York, NY 10018 or info@skyhorsepublishing.com.

Skyhorse® and Skyhorse Publishing® are registered trademarks of Skyhorse Publishing, Inc.®, a Delaware corporation.

Visit our website at www.skyhorsepublishing.com.

10 9 8 7 6 5 4 3 2

Library of Congress Cataloging-in-Publication Data is available on file.

Cover design by Tom Lau
Cover image credit: iStockphoto.com

Print ISBN: 978-1-5107-3868-3

Printed in China

Contents

Dedication

For the great times we have shared in the hunting woods, and for those memories that will last forever, I dedicate this book to my son, John Trout III.

Foreword

Since 1983, I have been an outdoor communicator. Besides hosting an outdoor TV show, I have written many magazine articles and authored more than a dozen books on white-tailed deer. Therefore, I am very familiar with outdoor print commentary. During my three-plus decades in the industry, I have had the pleasure of meeting, knowing, and befriending many of the nation's most prolific and knowledgeable authors of magazine articles and books. While many of them stand out as memorable journalists, one of them, the late John Trout, Jr. shines most brightly in my mind's eye.

Consider this: There are thousands of professional outdoor communicators within the outdoor industry, and many specialize in writing about white-tailed deer. Only a handful, however, have been able to achieve the kind of high regard from both their readers and peers as the late John Trout, Jr. did. John garnered his well-earned accolades not only through his skills and knowledge on all aspects of hunting whitetails, but also through his easy-to-read and understandable style of writing. What also made John impressive as a master deer hunter and communicator was that when his advice was put to the test in the field, it produced success for countless stump-sitters throughout the country.

Long before I became involved in a full-time outdoor career, I regularly read magazine articles (and books) about deer hunting strategies in what was known at the time as the "Big Three" magazines: *Field & Stream*, *Outdoor Life*, and *Sports Afield*. Time and time again, the deer-hunting articles in these publications that I consistently learned from and found most significant were penned by John Trout, Jr. His writings always contained concise, genuine, rock-solid information.

For decades, John Trout, Jr. was among the few *"preferred"* whitetail pros who were highly recognized by outdoor magazine editors. They turned to him to enhance the pages of their magazines with his deer-hunting knowledge. They entrusted John's material to take their readers' deer-hunting abilities to a higher level.

The simple fact about John Trout, Jr. was that his skills and understanding of the white-tailed deer were second to none. His writings have stood the most important and valuable test of all: time. John's recognition as a top-notch deer hunter and writer was justly earned. His distinction as an exceptional outdoor communicator on all things about white-tailed deer will shine brightly for decades to come.

I will state with certainty that anyone reading this book, be it a grizzled old-timer, a seasoned veteran, or a newbie to the sport of deer hunting, will benefit by acquiring first-class deer-hunting know-how from its pages.

When you are finished reading *Finding Wounded Deer*, you will have gained valuable information on something that can happen to any deer hunter. As John notes, we all hope to make a quick, clean kill. Sometimes, however, our shot can be a bit off, be it with bow or firearm. In such a situation, we need to know how to track and find a wounded deer. In this book, John tells you how to do it, how to interpret different types of wounds, and how to know what a wounded deer is likely to do and where it is likely to go.

I'm certain you will be so impressed with the late John Trout, Jr.'s writings, and that this book will find a permanent home in your hunting library. You will undoubtedly refer to it time and time again as the go-to information source for recovering a wounded deer.

Peter J. Fiduccia
a.k.a. The Deer Doctor
2019

Acknowledgements

Over the years, I have had the opportunity to track hundreds of wounded deer. I thank all those who helped me when I needed assistance, and all those who allowed me to assist them. There are far too many names to mention individually, but I am sure they know who they are. The tracking experiences I have shared with these people have made me a better hunter and tracker.

I express a special thanks to Dad, for introducing me to deer hunting, and for sharing his tracking expertise with me. He began deer hunting in the late 1950s, and gained valuable knowledge of this subject long before most of us knew what deer hunting was all about. At the time of this writing, he is 76 years young, and continues to hunt whitetails with bow and gun.

Thanks to my son John, for loving the great outdoors and sharing time there with me. I also thank my wife, Vikki, for her newfound interest in hunting, her support of this book, and for assisting with proofing the pages that follow.

I know tracking wounded deer is a touchy subject, with the antis and animal activists breathing down the necks of hunters, but many folks have considered the discussion of this subject necessary, so we can be responsible and ethical hunters. I thank them for doing so. There are Kate and Peter Fiduccia, who supported this book and inspired me to write the text that follows; numerous magazine editors and publishers who have had the courage to publish blood-trailing articles I have written; and those groups and organizations which allowed me to speak on the subject of tracking wounded deer at their events.

I also thank John Maltby, Supervisory Veterinary Medical Officer with the U.S. Dept. of Agriculture, for his comments. This qualified specialist sacrificed his busy time to make this a better book.

My good friend Larry Smail provided many of the illustrations in this book. I thank Larry for sharing his artistic abilities with you, and for getting them done at a moment's notice.

I thank Mike Coppola of Deer Search, Inc. for his comments, and all those members of the organization for their volunteer efforts locating wounded deer.

For permission to reprint illustrations and text, I thank the Wildlife Society, and the Wildlife Management Institute. The reprints are great assets to this book.

My first book about tracking wounded deer, *Trailing Whitetails*, was published many years ago and read by thousands of hunters. I thank all those readers for their comments and support. It made this book possible, and provided the inspiration for me to continue pursuit of this subject.

Finally, I thank God for being here, and for the hunting opportunities He has given me for so many years. Most of all, I thank Him for allowing me to see and enjoy His perfect creations, from the landscapes I have viewed, to the creatures I have come to know and understand.

Introduction

I seriously doubt that any topic is as interesting to deer hunters as tracking wounded deer, and rightfully so. This subject deserves special attention from all bow and gun hunters, both veterans and beginners, as well as all members of the outdoor trade that in one way or another rely on deer hunters for an income.

There are some who prefer not to discuss the topic of tracking wounded deer, for fear of exciting the anti-hunters and animal activists, or because they feel the topic doesn't matter. If you're reading this book you probably understand the importance of discussing wounded deer. It will better educate all of us, and will help to make us more responsible and ethical hunters.

No deer hunter looks forward to a long tracking job. We all hope for a quick, clean kill, but we know that sometimes the inevitable happens. Regardless of how well we shoot, our bullet or broadhead is sometimes off target. Everyone involved in deer hunting should also realize that tracking skills are only one of many phases involved in a hunt. Each phase determines just how effectively we hunt overall. We must retain woodsmanship ability, scout efficiently, know deer inside-and-out, have an understanding of our hunting equipment, be on target with bow or gun, and know how to recover a deer after making the shot.

My first book about wounded deer, *Trailing Whitetails*, was published in 1987. Putting together that book, and this book, took years of collecting photos and taking notes, and many months of writing. I've come a long way since the first tracking book, and have experienced numerous tracking endeavors since that time. I can honestly say that this second book about tracking deer shot with bow or gun is much better, and much more advanced, than the first.

This book provides many illustrations and photographs that are essential to its contents. They will give you a better understanding of the wounded deer, and provide you with a quick reference guide when you shoot a deer and need to know something right away.

Early in the book, you are reminded about the habits of wounded deer, why some common things occur after shooting a deer, and why some things happen that you do not expect. I also discuss blood trails that differ like night and day, and why some deer die quickly while others take hours to succumb.

You will read about the differences of bullet and arrow wounds, and the importance of knowing the kind of shot you made. Tips are also provided for tracking, whether you do or do not know what kind of hit you made. These tips are based on the color of blood. I discuss how you can read blood and the trail to help you determine how long to wait before you begin tracking.

Locations of hits, and tracking tips to support them, are broken into individual chapters. For instance, if you want to know more about a stomach-shot deer, you will find answers to your questions in the chapter titled "Abdominal Wounds." There are also chapters about cardiorespiratory, skeletal and muscle, and artery/vascular wounds. You will find that nothing is left out. You will read about every wound imaginable, from vital wounds such as lung and heart shots, to wounds where tallow and little or no blood is found. You may also be surprised to find out that some wounds are not considered superficial, even though you may have believed they were. In fact, you will discover that some wounds which you thought were superficial could actually result in a tagged deer if the right tracking techniques are employed.

One chapter dedicated to certain tracking occurrences. I experienced these over the years while tracking deer myself, or when assisting others. These real-life tracking events make great references. True, not all deer that encounter the same type of wound will react identically, but you may be surprised to discover the many similarities.

Finally, I think you'll appreciate the last chapter, which provides quick references for various types of wounds. These summaries tell you what to expect and how to track the deer without going back through the entire book and spending a lot of time attempting to find an answer to a particular dilemma. This section also comes in handy if you happen to have the book stuffed into a daypack while hunting.

As you might expect, this book contains a great deal of research. This research came from many individuals, other writers and books not necessarily based upon tracking, and veteran hunters who have been there. Also, John Maltby, Supervisory Veterinary Medical Officer with the U.S. Dept. of Agriculture, provided insight about some wounds that often leave us scratching our heads. The book is loaded with photos and illustrations that tell 1000 words.

This is not your everyday book of fireside tales. However, it will make you a better hunter and help you to recover more deer. Let's face it: Hunting is fun, but getting a deer is even more fun. Anti-hunters seem to think that deer hunting is similar to going out and shooting tin cans. We know better, and we know that it can be difficult to be successful, even on a good day in a great area. I don't know how seriously you take your deer hunting, but I do know that you will be a responsible hunter and have the best chance of finding the deer you shoot after reading this book. Enjoy.

John Trout, Jr.

Chapter 1

Wounded Deer Realities

On a chilly November evening during the late 1960s, a white-tailed doe passed by my stand. Not one to pass up a golden opportunity, I drew the string of my old Bear recurve bow, anchored, and released the fiberglass arrow. The dull thump that followed verified that my arrow had hit the deer in the body cavity. The following morning, I picked up the blood trail and tracked the wounded deer until the trail finally ended 250 yards from the thicket where the incident occurred. Although my search continued the rest of the day, I failed to find the deer.

Losing my first whitetail shot with bow and arrow was almost more than I could bear. It was frustrating, humiliating, heartbreaking and, well, you get the picture. Nevertheless, something good came out of this tracking endeavor. You see, from that day on I became obsessed with learning everything about the behavior and the recovery of wounded deer. I would make it a point to assist friends when tracking their deer, jumping at the chance to discover facts we knew little about.

Fortunately, today we know far more than we knew back then. I have now hunted whitetails with bow and gun for more than thirty-five years, and have participated in countless tracking pursuits. Many of these adventures ended with a filled tag. Some did not. However, all provided insights for future tracking efforts, and for the words contained within this book.

Today, the discussion of tracking wounded deer has become a hot topic. In fact, many publications that once refused to discuss the subject of tracking wounded deer now make it a point to include this subject regularly.

Before going on, let me first say that there is both good news and bad news about the coverage of tracking wounded deer. First comes the good news. Publications that do discuss the topic have done a great job of educating hunters. This is necessary as we continue to battle anti-hunters and animal activists, and further our need to learn about wounded deer.

I have often wished that it would be mandatory for hunters to pass a tracking and deer anatomy test before they could receive a deer hunting tag. Imagine if everyone received a booklet with anatomy illustrations, shot placement tips, guidelines for determining hits, and tracking and recovery tactics. Each license applicant would have to study the booklet, then take a basic test. Some people might disagree with this idea, but I see it as a gateway to building more responsible hunters. The more we know about the subject of tracking deer, the better we are prepared to stand up to the antis and activists, the better ethics we will practice, the better shots we will take, and the more deer we will recover.

A bowhunting instructor in Iowa once told me that we must continue educational practices about shooting and tracking deer. He based his opinion on how little some hunters know about whitetail anatomy. One student, who viewed a large illustration of a white-tailed buck, was asked to point out the location of the animal's heart. He selected a spot at the base of the neck where it joins the shoulders. Many students were also surprised to learn about the precise location of the lungs, and had no idea that the lungs of an adult deer were nine inches in diameter.

Now let's get back to the coverage of wounded deer that has taken place in recent years. The bad news is that some writers have misled hunters. Now don't get me wrong, most who write about tracking wounded deer have a good understanding of the subject, and they have done a great job of informing readers. Some, however, did not get the facts straight before passing them along. For instance, one writer who discussed tracking gut-shot deer talked about a kidney hit and compared it to the liver and stomach wound. He claimed a kidney-shot deer would die in a few hours and would bleed very slowly internally. Unfortunately, he failed to realize how much blood flows through the kidneys. A hole in the kidneys causes immediate hemorrhage and death within seconds.

Once a hunter shoots, he has an ethical responsibility to do everything he can to recover the animal.

Other writers have passed along opinions taken from hunter surveys. While statistical information is interesting and sometimes helpful, it does not necessarily tell the whole story. In other words, 500 hunters may give opinions and make guesses to some tracking questions. But consider that many of these 500 hunters may not be very experienced. Some may have tracked only one or two deer; others may have simply misread the questions, and thus answered incorrectly.

I don't claim to know all there is about tracking wounded deer. I keep an open mind and seem to learn something new each time an experience occurs. I also absorb the information I read and give it careful consideration. However, I cannot deny the cliche, "Experience is the best teacher."

Since I have always kept records of hunts, harvests, and tracking occurrences, I have been able to come up with a few interesting and helpful facts. In the past thirty-seven years, I have participated in more than 450 tracking events. Many were deer I have shot, many were deer shot by other hunters. Approximately 300 of these incidents occurred before 1985. Since that time, my tracking pursuits have decreased simply because these days I pass on more shots, holding out for a trophy.

I have seen every wound imaginable, and have seen the unexpected occur on many occasions. Nonetheless, these experiences have helped me to recover many wounded deer. Some were recovered only because others, or I, recognized a certain wound and knew how the animal would react. Yes, I have been fortunate to have the assistance of many friends who know the ins-and-outs of tracking wounded deer. The primary objective is to tag a deer. That's what we all want to do. However, I'm like you, in that I enjoy the hunt. I love to see a beautiful sunrise and sunset, watch all the critters running around the woods, learn the habits of the deer I watch, and just love to feel and breath country air.

However, I doubt any of us will deny the bottom line. We want to kill a deer no matter how much we enjoy the additional pleasures that come with a quality hunt. As I have said before, the kill is like the icing on the cake.

Shot Placement

Of course, before any of us can feel the excitement of a kill, we must first have a good understanding of a deer's anatomy. We must know where to place the broadhead or bullet, and we must know what shots we should and should not take

There are a few golden rules to remember about shooting at a deer: You must judge yardage with some degree of accuracy and avoid shooting beyond your effective shooting range; you must wait until the animal offers a shot that allows you to make a clean kill; you should shoot only when you are confident of killing the deer; and you must know the precise location of the vital organs if you are to accomplish anything.

Despite these facts, some hunters still take unwarranted shots. Others have also gotten the idea, perhaps from a previous thrilling experience, that they should not shoot at the lungs of a deer - the animal's largest vitals. For instance, I often hear from hunters who prefer to shoot at the heart. Why would anyone prefer to shoot for the heart when the lungs are much larger and may put the animal down as quickly, and sometimes sooner? Another guy told me he always shoots for the neck. He relies on hitting a two-inch-diameter vertebrate, or perhaps the one-half-inch carotid artery, to put the deer down, instead of the nine-inch diameter lungs. Maybe

Deer hunters should take only those shots they believe will result in quick, clean kills. This buck is quartering away, allowing plenty of room for a bullet or broadhead to reach the vitals.

this guy shot a deer in the neck once and dropped it immediately. Maybe he did it twice. Maybe the first time he hit the deer in the neck it was totally accidental. Who knows? But I do know that it makes no sense to select a small target when a bigger target exists. I also know that it is easy for a projectile or broadhead to miss the vitals in the neck and pass through only muscle.

Each hunter must know his equipment and its capabilities. He should also realize the best shot is a broadside or slightly quartering-away shot. Quartering away is best because it allows room for error. Your broadhead or bullet is heading for the vital area. Never consider taking quartering-into and facing-into shots unless the an mal is close and you know beyond any doubt that your broadhead or projectile can hit a vital organ. Sometimes it is possible, sometimes it isn't.

A two-season hunter must also know when one weapon will get the job done and another will not. For instance, I will not hesitate to shoot at the shoulder of a deer when I'm using a firearm and the animal presents the perfect opportunity. However, although a few of my arrows have passed through the shoulder blade of a deer and reached the lungs, I make it a point to keep my sights focused behind the shoulder of the animal when bowhunting.

Broadheads and Bullets

Speaking of broadheads and bullets, both are effective when the hunter takes a preferred shot. But there are certain limitations that apply to a bowhunter that may not apply to a firearm hunter. Bone is of primary concern. It has nothing to do with hemorrhage and tissue damage. A razor-sharp broadhead is lethal and, when coupled with the right bow, arrow, and hunter, will usually penetrate completely and kill quickly. In fact, I have found in most cases, when identical wounds exist, the right broadhead produces a better blood trail than a projectile does.

Your choice of broadheads should be taken seriously, however. Although I hunt with bow and gun, I have always had a stronger love for the archery season. Over the years, I have tried countless brands of broadheads in the backyard and in the field. I have found that inconsistent arrow flight and poor blood trails exist from broadhead to broadhead. This should concern all bowhunters. Most of us realize that some broadheads do not fly like field points, and we realize that some cannot be easily tuned. However, the big test occurs when you shoot a deer. You could say that some have it, and some do not. We know a sharp broadhead is necessary, but it's also a fact that even some razor-sharp broadheads are responsible for poor blood trails. It's really a test all bowhunters must go through. All broadheads can kill, but you must still discover those that shoot best, and those broadheads that do the damage you expect.

Every hunter must also realize that blood trails are not always dependent upon the projectile or broadhead used. Poor blood trails are often the result of the wound location. I have shot deer in the stomach with one-ounce slugs and found no blood on the ground. The same has happened when using sharp broadheads. This is common, because organ tissue often clogs the entry and departure holes.

The height of the entry and departure hole will also affect the amount of blood that gets to the ground. With this in mind, the hunter must always consider the wound before he decides that his equipment was responsible for a poor blood trail.

The size and weight of the bullet and broadhead may or may not have an effect on the blood trail. You must decide for yourself what works best and what will increase your chances of recovering an animal after the shot. Any projectile and broadhead will kill when it passes through the vitals, but some do it quicker than others, and some do more damage and result in better blood trails.

When hunting with a muzzleloader, I have sacrificed the fine accuracy of some projectiles and went with others that made bigger holes and left better blood trails. These bullets could not group in a one-inch circle at 100 yards, but they can group in a four-inch circle at seventy-five yards. Since my shots are usually fifty yards or less when deer hunting, I go with the projectile that does the most damage, yet has enough accuracy and size to get the job done.

In recent years, bowhunters have seen the introduction of many new types of broadheads. Some have large cutting diameters and some do not. However, a broadhead with a large cutting diameter is not necessarily the best to use. We have also had the opportunity to try mechanical broadheads - made to open on impact. In my opinion, mechanical broadheads are still going through the testing period. Some manufacturers introduced these heads because they felt it necessary to keep up with the competition. Some hunters claim mechanical heads are the greatest, while others claim penetration is severely affected. Again, it comes down to trying what works best for you. Personally, I stick with the common theory: If it ain't broke, don't fix it. If you are dissatisfied with a particular tracking endeavor and believe your broadheads could be to blame, try to find something better. If you like the results of what you have, keep using them.

When a non-vital wound occurs, hunters often wonder which causes the most trauma and damage to tissue - broadheads or projectiles. Although one could come to various conclusions, depending upon the precise location of a non-vital wound, and the broadhead or bullet that hits a deer, it has been determined that less tissue damage and trauma occurs from a sharp broadhead. However, research has determined that many wounded deer that are not found, do recover, regardless of whether the hunter shot the animal with a bow or gun. In fact, if organs are spared and infection is not a factor, a deer will recover.

During the past three decades, I have witnessed the recovery of several deer with previous wounds. These wounds appeared to range from one week to one year old. Most of the deer had previous wounds to a leg, shoulder, or neck.
One incident in particular involved a small buck I shot with a bow straight down under my tree stand. The arrow slid along the inside of the rib cage, but apparently missed the vital lungs. We tracked the deer about 100 yards until the blood trail ceased. After a careful search in the hours that followed, I finally gave up the trail. One year later, a friend of mine killed the buck in the same area. We found a six-inch piece of my unmistakable arrow shaft, and the broadhead inside the animal's chest when we field dressed the deer. Tissue had formed around the shaft and

broadhead, and the deer appeared healthy.

Be Persistent

Getting back to the realities of wounded deer, we must realize that some deer do not die. Superficial wounds occur, even when an obvious blood trail may lead you to believe otherwise. You will need to know the difference in wounds that are only superficial and those that will result in the deer succumbing. Equally important, however, is realizing you have an ethical responsibility to do everything you can to recover an animal, despite any belief that the wound is superficial or otherwise. You will feel better with yourself if you do everything you can to recover an animal, even if it is lost in the end. As long as you can see a blood trail, and up to a certain period after the blood trail is lost, the hunter must put a strong effort into recovering the animal. Many hunters recover their deer only because they did not give up. It is not always an obvious blood trail that leads them to the downed deer, but simply a determination to keep looking.

To fulfill our ethical responsibility, the hunter must first consider the little things that begin the moment he pulls the trigger or releases the bowstring. You must watch the animal closely to see how it leaves the scene. Did it run or walk away? Did it stop and stand in one spot? Exactly which direction did it go? Surprisingly, being aware of these little things could make the difference in recovering or not recovering the animal.

Then comes the waiting game. You must know how long to wait before you begin tracking. Tracking too quickly, or too late, could make the difference in finding a downed deer, or causing a deer to go down. Different wounds require different waiting periods. Sometimes it is better to push the deer and other times it is better to wait for minutes, or even several hours, before you begin tracking.

Despite the hours of scouting and pursuing it takes to finally get a shot at that certain deer, you may also find yourself needing tracking skills before the hunt ends. It's the last phase of a successful hunt.

Finally, it comes down to tracking skills. You must know what to look for, and where you will find valuable sign that could lead you to the deer. Will the deer bed down or will it run or walk until it drops? Some blood trails are sparse while others are easy to follow. What does it mean when you find blood in a pool and what does it mean when only droplets or smears are found? Yes, many questions come up when you discuss tracking a wounded deer. The following chapters will provide the answers and solutions to these questions, and more. All hunters wonder what their chances are of recovering a deer they shot. Certainly, the possibility of a recovery depends upon several factors that you are probably aware of. However, to gain a little insight, one could consider one of the few wounded deer studies conducted in North America.

The Camp Ripley Study

During four bowhunts at Camp Ripley, Minnesota from 1992 - 93, research officials did an extensive wounded deer study. The study was conducted by Jay McAninch and Wendy Krueger of the Minnesota DNR, Dr. Dave Samuel of West Virginia University, and several colleagues.

After the interviews and statistics were completed, it was determined that archers reported hitting 955 deer. Interestingly, 693 bowhunters, or 86.8 percent retrieved a deer. Surprisingly, only thirteen percent of the deer wounded were not recovered.

Also worth mentioning is the fact that Camp Ripley bowhunters apparently picked their shots wisely during the four hunts. Of the total archers that shot deer, and interviewed by trained officials when they checked out, sixty-six percent said they took "Broadside" shots, while twenty-eight percent claimed they took "Quartering" shots (quartering into and quartering away). Only a small percentage of the hunters said they took "Head-on," Straight-Away," and "Straight Down" shots.

In ending this chapter and the final mention of our responsibility as a hunter, each of us must consider his or her actions and how they will reflect on all hunters. Non-hunters, even those that are not anti-hunters, don't want to hear about deer we did not recover. The Camp Ripley study certainly proved positive for hunters and negative for animal activists who have claimed that hunters are losing a large percentage of deer they wound. Certainly, bad hits are occasionally going to happen. We are human and we do make mistakes. Nonetheless, most of us do take warranted shots and recover most wounded deer.

A hunter once told me he had never lost a deer. I must believe he hasn't hunted too long. Anyone who hunts long enough with bow or gun is going to lose an animal someday, even if he shoots accurately and is the best tracker of the area. Regardless of whether you are a beginning deer hunter or a veteran, you will decrease the risk of losing an animal after reading the pages that follow.

	1992		1993		
	Hunt 1	Hunt 2	Hunt 3	Hunt 4	Average
Total Deer Hit	331	219	266	139	238.8
Retrieved Deer	248	158	190	97	173.3
Recovery Rate (%)	92.2	83.2	87.6	84.3	86.8
Loss Rate (%)	7.8	16.8	12.4	15.7	13.2

Table Camp Ripley: Total deer hit and retrieved at Camp Ripley, Minnesota during 1992 - 1993.

Chapter 2

Analyzing the Shot

Before tracking, a hunter should analyze what happened right after the shot. These details are of little importance if the deer drops in its tracks, but can make a huge difference if the deer ran or walked away from the area when hit. The hunter must then decipher the rest of the puzzle, beginning with knowing whether he hit or missed his target.

Reactions of Deer

Consider the hunter who suffered from extreme anxiety when the deer approached to within thirty yards. He nervously and instinctively shouldered his rifle, and then squeezed the trigger. As the deer ran off, he stood in his stand and attempted to figure out exactly what had happened. He could hardly remember shooting and, once on the ground, had no idea where the deer had been standing moments earlier.

Even if the hunter scanned a large area looking for sign, he probably wouldn't be in the right place. He can't remember how the deer reacted to the shot, and has no idea if he hit the deer, or the type of wound he is dealing with. The situation now looks grim, and the chance of a quick, clean recovery appears slim. This scenario happens quite a bit. Many hunters fail to notice what goes on after the shot, and have no idea if they even hit their intended target. This usually leads them to look for their deer prematurely, which can result in pushing away an animal that might have been recovered. The fact is, many deer shot with bow or gun do not always show definite signs of being hit. However, the observant hunter will always notice a few of the finer details, details which can reveal if the deer was hit.

A deer's reaction to a shot varies. Of particular importance are the location of the wound and the nervousness of the animal when the shot was fired will affect its reaction.

Several years ago, my son John prepared to shoot as a nervous doe walked within easy bow range. She spotted his movement and looked up at the tree stand where he was perched. By this time John had already drawn, anchored, and settled his sights behind the doe's shoulder. He released and watched the arrow cleanly pass through the doe's lungs. The deer turned sharply and ran for thirty yards before stopping. Then she turned around, looked back, and snorted. She lunged forward a few yards and fell dead,

Another hunter I know spotted a deer in a food plot made a cautious stalk until he was within easy gun range. Moments later, the rifle roared and the buck jumped straight up in the air, indicating it had been hit. However, the buck did not take off rapidly. Instead, it stood there a couple of seconds, staring across the field, then put its head down and resumed feeding. As the shocked hunter prepared to shoot again, the deer suddenly dropped to its front knees. A second or two later, it rolled onto its side and took a few last kicks. The hunter later discovered he had made a perfect lung shot.

The reactions of these deer were unusual, but they demonstrate that unusual circumstances can happen. Most often, a lung-shot deer will turn and run away at break-neck speed, or sometimes drop instantly when the shoulder is hit. These deer did not, even though one of them had detected the hunter just before the shot.

Most wounded whitetails run away with their tails down. This is particularly true of those that are hit hard. Exceptions always exist, however. Some deer, when shot, only lope off and flag their tail side-to-side, as they would do when spooked from a bed. This is rare, but it does happen. Interestingly, the location of the wound may play a role in the deer's reaction to being hit.

Most wounded whitetails leave the scene with their tail tucked. There are always exceptions to the rule, however. For this reason, never assume you missed just because the tail was up.

For instance, most paunch-shot deer I have observed loped away, and seldom flagged their tail. In fact, when a whitetail does the unexpected and flags its tail, it is usually one that has been hit in the vitals. About ninety percent of the deer I have seen that were shot in the heart, lungs, or both, ran away with their tail tucked. The remaining ten percent flagged and did not run as hard as those that kept their tail tucked. No one knows why these incidents happen.

Wounds to bones or muscles usually send a deer running away hard, with their tail tucked. Seldom do these deer lope away with their tail flagging, even if the wound is only superficial.

It's important to understand the difference between bullet and broadhead wounds. The bullet produces shocking power and trauma, and does some damage to tissue, blood vessels, and organs. A bowhunter relies exclusively on a sharp broadhead and the damage it does to tissue, blood vessels, and organs.

The shocking power of a bullet often knocks a deer to the ground, even when the shoulder blade is untouched. It's also true that shock may cause a deer to stay down temporarily, or permanently. Temporary shock can often cost a hunter, however.

On one occasion, I shot a huge eleven-pointer at sixty yards with a slug gun. I later learned that the slug passed through the base of the neck where it joins the shoulder, missing the vertebrate. However, when the deer dropped and lay motion-less for five minutes, I believed the slug had probably hit the shoulder or spine. As I was on the way out of the tree, I spotted the deer beginning to move. Just as I reached the ground, the buck was on its feet, staggering away but gaining momen-tum with every second that passed by. Another hunter downed the deer a few min-utes later, and I assumed that shock was the only thing that probably kept the deer down after I had shot.

Many bullet wounds result in shock to deer, even if the projectile does not hit vitals. Heavy projectiles, particularly those that expand, seem to hit the hard-est and induce the most shock. That is not to say that the heaviest bullets are best to use, however. It only means that we may notice a deer's reaction to a heavier projectile more often than we notice a reaction to a lighter bullet. Keep in mind, bone and heavy muscle usually cause a projectile to expand more than softer areas such as the paunch. Additionally, rib bones are soft and seldom cause a bullet to expand as much as those that hit other bones or heavy muscle.

One shocking (I mean that literally) story I heard involved a Kentucky hunter who participated at a random-draw hunt. He knocked down a buck the first morning with his rifle, climbed down from his stand, and walked away to get his buddy. The two returned and began shooting photos as the proud hunter stood behind the deer and laid his rifle across the huge antlers of the buck. A couple of camera clicks later, the deer came to life, sprung to his feet, and bounded away. Neither hunter ever saw the deer again.

Is this story true? I don't know. Hearsay is usually interesting but the facts are sometimes twisted. Is it possible? Yes.

**Blood is not always present at the location
the deer stood when you took the shot. Still,
a deer will usually leave scuffed areas on the
ground when it tears away quickly.**

Shock can occur long after a deer endures an arrow or bullet wound. However, I have also seen deer go into immediate shock due to arrow wounds. A Pennsylvania buck, that I hit high in the back lay almost motionless when I approached some fifteen minutes after the shot. As I got within a few feet of the downed animal, it slowly got up and walked away, staggering with each step. Regulations did not allow me to carry a bow as I tracked the deer in the dark, so I could only watch as the deer moved away. The following day, I jumped the deer from its bed and it ran away, very alert. Eventually, the wound proved to be only superficial.

I know of two other loin-shot deer that were hit with arrows that seemed to go into temporary shock just moments after the shot. Paunch-shot deer, on the other hand, never seem to go into an immediate, paralyzing shock, nor do those hit in the vitals.

Some hunters may be more impressed with a gun wound, solely because of the knockdown power. However, this has little to do with overall damage. The sharp broadhead causes hemorrhaging that cannot be matched by a projectile. As mentioned in the previous chapter, the right broadhead is as lethal as any bullet.

I have already talked about deer running hard when shot. This is particularly common of deer that are not hit in the paunch. When a hit deer runs hard, it usually has its belly low to the ground and appears to be setting a new sprint record for the 100-yard dash. Another indication of a deer being wounded is that it will pass over the top of obstacles. I have seen them crash through brushpiles and other major debris that they would bypass any other time when fleeing from a bed after being jumped. Who knows what is going on in their mind, if anything? However, I must believe that they know survival is at stake when the wound occurs.

If you shoot at a deer that is with other deer, it will usually break away from the others shortly after leaving the scene. It may run with them a short distance, but the wounded deer will probably turn away and travel a different direction.

You can safely assume a deer is wounded if it beds down within view of your ambush site. If you see the deer bed down, you should stay put, watch the deer closely, and let it make the next move.

A deer that leaves the scene and beds down within view is probably wounded. Deer often bed down when shot in the liver, stomach, or intestines. However, other wounds may also induce bedding close to the shot location. This commonly occurs when the deer does not know the hunter is there, but sometimes will happen even when it is sure of the hunter's presence. If you see a deer bed down, I would suggest you stay put and watch the deer closely. The idea is to let it make the next move. You can safely assume you have wounded the deer, and the last thing you want to do is send it running away to parts unknown.

Precise Locations

The hunter must make a mental note of the area right after the shot. The precise location where the animal stood is crucial when you attempt to decipher what happened, and you try to find blood. The further away you are from the location, the more difficult it may be to find the exact location.

The location of the wound has a lot to do with how the deer reacts after the shot. Deer hit in the vital organs, bone, or heavy muscle usually leave the scene rapidly. Paunch-shot deer often lunge forward, run a short distance, and begin walking.

Always pinpoint landmarks that you can search for later. Such a landmark may be a rock, a certain tree, or perhaps a little thicket. It is probably easier to make a mental note of a location if you are in a tree stand when the shot is taken, but even an observant ground hunter can get close to the precise location where the deer once stood.

If anxiety clouds your awareness and prevents your seeing the precise location, take notice of the direction in which the deer walked or ran after the shot, and anything it passed by. Being close is better than not knowing at all. You can also assume that the precise location will look different from afar than up close. If this happens and you can't find the location, return to your original ambush site and look again. This tactic has helped many hunters on countless occasions to find the precise location where the deer stood, or the direction in which it ran. I have often returned to my tree stand to look over the area when I couldn't find blood sign or tracks.

Any deer that does not drop will usually kick up leaves at the location where the shot occurred. A careful examination of the area will reveal kicked-up leaves or debris, and sometimes tracks. Tracks may not appear as they do normally, however. The tracks of a deer that has fled from the scene usually appear as scuffed or scraped areas in the soil.

Always mark the location where the deer stood when the shot was taken. White toilet paper shows up better than clothing, or the accessories you carry.

Once you find the precise location where you shot the deer, or where it left the area, mark it with something that is easy to see. Bright tissue paper hung on limbs about shoulder height works well, and you can see it for a long distance. I usually tear off one- to two-foot-long piece that can dangle loosely. Remember to remove the tissue paper after you have finished tracking the deer, or if you have determined a miss. The second best thing you can use is trail-marking ribbon. Camouflage hats, bows, guns, fanny packs, and other hunting accessories do not work as well as markers, even during daylight. If you do not have anything with you to mark the spot, clear a large bare spot on the ground. This will be easy to find if you return to the shot location.

Arrow and Projectile Analysis

Unlike the bowhunter who may retrieve an arrow and determine a hit or miss, the firearm hunter cannot rely on positive evidence, such as a clean or bloody arrow. However, the firearm hunter can look for shattered limbs and trees that may have marks which indicate a miss. On some occasions, after not finding blood, I have returned to the location where the deer was standing and analyzed the path of my projectile. Sometimes, I could find the spot where the deer tore away, and then locate something the projectile struck. A bullet that hits a tree or a large limb is sure to do some damage. All you have to do is find it.

A few years ago, during Indiana's muzzleloader season, a buck approached within thirty yards of my tree stand. The respectable eight-pointer walked broad-side to me, offering a perfect shot. The crosshairs of my scope settled on the deer's shoulder and I squeezed the trigger. When the smoke cleared, I could see the buck running off with its tail flagging. Knowing I could not have missed, I climbed down and found where the deer had been standing before it left the scene. Immediately, I could see a large clump of hair, apparently from the brisket of the deer. I could also see scuff marks in the leaves. However, a futile search revealed no blood or deer.

After I returned with friends later in the morning, I climbed back into the tree stand to look over the area in an attempt to pinpoint the deer's travel direction when it left. To my amazement, I could see a huge, shattered limb in a white pine only ten yards in front of my stand, about fifteen feet above the ground. Then I knew what had happened. The projectile had deflected after slicing through the limb, probably hitting the deer on the underneath side of its brisket, resulting in only a superficial wound. In fact, I could then remember seeing the limb in the scope before shooting. I had raised the gun slightly to miss the limb, but in doing so put it in the way of the projectile.

The bowhunter, if he or she does not see the arrow in the deer, usually looks for it beyond the location where the deer was standing. Following the flight of an arrow is not always possible and attempting to do so can lead to a poor follow-through and missed shot. Of course, an arrow may also deflect before it reaches a deer, and might not be found anywhere close. However, common sense usually has us looking for the arrow beyond the location where the deer stood.

Upon finding the spent arrow, look it over for blood. If it is covered on all sides with blood, it usually signifies a pass-through. Be aware, though, that debris, particularly wet foliage, may clean an arrow of some or all of the blood. For this reason, a thorough examination is necessary before making a final determination.

The location of the wound will also determine how much blood will be on the arrow shaft. For instance, an arrow that passes through the paunch of a deer may have little or no blood on the shaft, and perhaps only a small amount of tissue. The same goes for an arrow that merely grazes a deer, or deflects on bone. Every bowhunter should look at an arrow very closely, and do it under a light whenever possible.

The author examines his arrow for blood, tissue, or tallow. In rare situations, wet foliage and debris can wipe an arrow almost clean. Always examine a spent arrow carefully in good light to determine if you hit or missed. (Photo by Vikki L. Trout.)

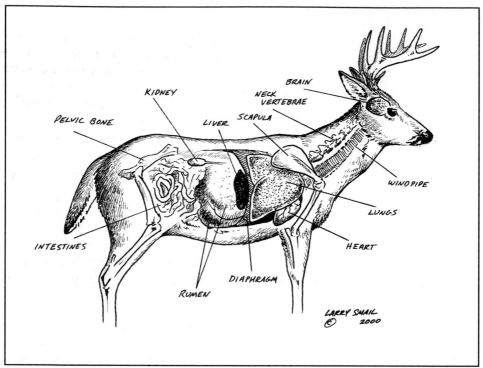

The hunter has an ethical responsibility to know the anatomy of a deer, and to take only those shots that will kill cleanly and quickly. Only then can he become a skillful tracker when a deer is wounded, and travels farther than anticipated.

My dad once shot at a doe that showed no signs of being wounded. He climbed down from his tree, found his spent arrow, examined it, and climbed back up in the tree convinced he had missed. As he sat there for awhile holding his bow, he began to see traces of what first appeared to be tallow on the shaft. Looking more closely, he determined it was stomach tissue. Additionally, he smelled an odor on the shaft.

This story had a successful conclusion. Knowing the arrow had passed through the paunch of the deer, he waited a few hours, then started tracking, soon picking up a few drops of blood a short distance from where the deer stood when he released the arrow. Following the trail slowly, he found the doe 150 yards away where she had bedded down and died.

Both projectiles and broadheads may cut hair, and you may find hair at the precise location the deer stood. When found, it is usually positive evidence of a wound. Thus, if you cannot determine whether you have hit or missed the deer, look over the ground closely. Deer hair tells a very interesting story, as you have read in the previous chapter. Deer hair varies in size, texture, and color throughout the animal's body. For this reason, a close examination of deer hair may even tell you the location of the wound.

Sound Advice

Certain sounds may also offer positive evidence of a hit or miss. For instance, when an arrow hits the body cavity of a deer (the area behind the shoulder and in front of the hips), it usually produces a dull thump. Arrows that hit limbs or trees often produce a loud crack. This sound is similar to the sounds of an arrow that hits bone, but there is a distinct difference between the two.

When an arrow hits bone, the sound is usually sharper than the sound of an arrow hitting limbs. This is particularly true of shoulder blades and leg bones. Ribs may cause a slight cracking sound, but it is much duller than the sound of a shattering shoulder blade or leg bone.

If there is plenty of distance between the shooter and the deer (200 yards or more), a projectile may be heard hitting the animal. Usually, that sound is a dull thump.

In conclusion, I would suggest that every hunter always think positive after shooting at a deer. You must believe your shot was on target. by doing so, you are sure to spend more time looking for sign that will determine whether you really hit or missed it. In fact, you should never give up looking until you are sure beyond any doubt that you missed. I don't have a problem with any hunter who fails to recover a deer they shot. Sometimes this can't be helped, and anyone can hit a deer poorly. However, assuming a miss without a careful examination, only to discover otherwise a few days later, is sure to be detrimental to our sport.

© **Ted Rose**

Chapter 3

Reading Deer Hair

Throughout this book, I stress the importance of locating hair and reading it closely to determine the type of wound you are dealing with. I provide descriptions of deer hair in this chapter, each of the chapters that discuss precise wounds, and in the last chapter. I did so for three reasons: 1) It is often the first sign you will find after the shot; 2) It may be the only sign you will find; and 3) It may help you to determine how you should go about tracking the deer.Deer change color during the course of the year, as the hair is shed or thickened. In summer, it has a reddish shade, while in winter it has a grayish cast. The time of year for color change depends upon the latitude, the sub-species of deer, and the physical condition of the animal.

The winter coat is shed in the spring, and can be spotted by observant the outdoorsman. When scouting and turkey hunting during spring, I have found large bunches in one clump, then a little farther down the trail another clump. It is common to find shed hair if you are in deer country during spring. The deer hunter should mainly be concerned with the winter coat. Many times you can spot deer just beginning to change to a winter coat in early fall. Some deer may still have reddish spots in November, while others will already be gray.

The winter hair is hollow and filled with air for better insulation against the cold and to keep the deer somewhat waterproof. To retain even more heat, the winter coats of deer in northern latitudes are also darker than those of southern deer. The deer's winter hair is generally dark gray and grayish-brown at the tip, although there are variations.

It is important for the hunter to know what color hair comes from what part of the body. The color and thickness does change slightly at different points of the body. There are also whitish areas around the eyes and muzzle, inside the ears, on the throat, rump and belly, down the inside of each leg and, of course, on the under side of the tail of the white-tailed deer.

Several years ago a hunter who had just come out from a morning's hunt advised me that there was a white deer in the area. Since I always enjoy seeing these rare beauties, I asked where. He said he did not see the deer itself, but that he had found white hair on a barbed-wire fence.

The poor guy is probably now aware of how foolish he sounded, and hopefully he has learned that all whitetails have some white hair. All deer hunters should familiarize themselves with the winter coat, as many times hair will be the only thing they find at the scene where the deer was shot.

An arrow slices off hair as soon as it enters a deer's hide, and if it is a pass-through, the hunter will find hair on his broadhead and arrow shaft. Whether a pass-through or not, you can usually count on finding a few hairs. Normally, you won't find a large quantity. If you do find a large clump of hair, however, then the possibility exists that your arrow ran along the side of the deer.

One of the most intriguing trailing jobs I have ever been on was due to finding a large amount of hair on the ground. My friend shot a doe when it bedded down a short distance from his tree stand. The arrow had evidently sliced the deer for several inches along the body. Hair was all over the ground, and a blind man could almost have followed the blood trail, which we found for better than a mile in the dark before we were forced to give it up. We never located this deer, but when I look back, I wish we had pursued it a bit more that night. Had we continued to slowly push the doe and keep it moving, we might have caused enough blood loss so it would have gone down. It was one of those hits you could swear severed an artery. However, as most experienced trackers know, external blood seldom has much to do with causing an animal to succumb.

I like to keep a buck's winter coat on hand for inspecting hair I find from wounded deer. It comes in handy to compare the sample hair to the rug hair. However, if you do the same, make sure you don't leave the hide on the floor, since a winter coat of hollow hair is very brittle and breaks off easily. A deer hide left on the floor will not last long, nor will a hide that's constantly exposed to sunlight. Sunlight will bleach out the hair in a very short time..

Finding hair on the ground has helped my tracking efforts on numerous occasions, but one incident in particular stands out. It was the third day of Indiana's firearm season. I was in a tree stand overlooking a line of rubs and scrapes that I had hunted during the early bow season without much luck. About an hour before dark, the wind picked up and a cold front started moving in. I was not dressed for the weather, but I decided to stay in the tree anyway.

About thirty minutes before dark, I saw movement to my left. Since the wind was blowing hard, hearing was nearly impossible. I did not see anything plainly, and I delayed reaching for my gun that was hanging on a limb. Suddenly, a buck came into view out of a thicket only twenty yards from my stand. As I slowly reached for my gun, the buck threw its head up and stared at me for what seemed an eternity. Finally, it lowered its head back to level ground, evidently content that I was nothing to worry about. I slowly inched the gun to my shoulder and buried my open sights on his left front shoulder, which was angled slightly toward me. I really didn't want to shoot at that angle, but the buck didn't move, perhaps feeling certain that something was just not right. Taking a breath, I squeezed the trigger and the shotgun slug roared toward its destination. Then the buck turned and loped away with his tail flagging, showing absolutely no sign of being hit.

At first, I couldn't believe my eyes. Had I really missed at twenty yards? As I sat in my stand with darkness fast approaching, impatience got the best of me and I climbed down to take a look at the ground. I could find nothing where the deer had been standing. I next searched in the direction the buck had gone, but found no blood there either. Finally, using my flashlight at this point, I went back to the spot where the buck had been standing and got down on my hands and knees. There, I found about a half-dozen hairs, convincing me of a hit. At home I was able to identify the hair as coming from the shoulder area, predicting a possible good hit.

I went back early the next morning, crawling on my hands and knees for better than an hour, looking for blood. I could find nothing. I knew that a deer hit through the shoulder should not go far, especially if both lungs were hit, so I walked ahead in the direction the buck had taken. Within seventy yards I found the seven-pointer. The slug had entered high on the right shoulder, and taken out both lungs, but had failed to exit.

I was lucky to have found that buck; maybe not that I found it, but fortunate that I found the hair. Without it, I might have assumed a miss and the buck could have wasted away. Obviously, a hunter should never assume he missed until he has made a thorough search for any and all sign that would indicate a hit. In fact, always check the area where the deer stood when you took the shot, and for a considerable distance that the deer traveled before assuming a miss. Give up looking only when there is no doubt that you missed.

The importance of looking for hair and reading it after you find it cannot be overemphasized. It can help determine that you have made a hit, and also where.

It can be difficult to look at the hair and determine what might represent an entry or exit hole. If you are sure of the deer's angle when it was shot, however, then you might be able to determine which comes from where, particularly if you are fortunate to find hair from two different body locations.

Identification Guide to Deer Hair

1. **Stomach or Side Hair** - Coarse with lighter tips than chest hair, two to two and a half inches long.
2. **Navel Hair** - White and very coarse, hollow, curly and twisted, and longer than stomach hair.
3. **Spine Hair** - Very coarse, hollow, dark gray with black tips, two and a half to two and three-quarter inches long.
4. **Top of Back Hair** - Very coarse, hollow, dark gray with black tips, but slightly shorter than spine hair.
5. **Ham Hair** - Very coarse, dark brown or gray with black tips, but only about two inches long.
6. **Lower Leg Hair** - Very coarse, dark brown or gray, but only about one and a half inches long.
7. **Hair between Hind Legs** - Not hollow and very fine, white and silky, curly and about two inches long.
8. **Heart and Lung Hair** - Coarse, dark brown or gray with black tips, two and a quarter to two and three-quarter inches long.
9. **Brisket** - Very coarse, light or dark gray with dark tips, very stiff but may curl, two and a half to two and three-quarter inches long.

10. **Neck Hair** - Very fine, light gray, one and a half to one and three-quarter inches long.

11. **Tail Hair** - Coarse on top, dark brown or gray with dark tips, wavy and about two and a half to two and three-quarter inches long. Finer on underneath of tail, white and wavy, about two and a half to two and three-quarter inches long.

If there are plenty of leaves in the area where the deer was standing when you shot, pick them up individually and carefully turn them over. You will be surprised how much easier it is to see hair instead of just looking over a large section of leaves. Be sure to bend over closely to the ground, and get on your hands and knees if necessary. Always use caution when you get down on all fours, since this may disrupt hair on the ground.

Deer hair is just as important as a blood trail, so I would suggest you put as much interest in finding it as you do blood. There are times when I know I made a good hit, and couldn't care less about a few hairs, but there are other times when finding just a few hairs has lead me to a downed deer.

© **Ted Rose**

© Ted Rose

Chapter 4

Before the Shot

Over the years, I've seen a few magazine articles titled "After the Shot." These stories focused on recovering a deer once the animal is hit. Nonetheless, if you stop and think about the efforts that will go into recovering a deer with a particular wound, it begins before you shoot. The moment you release the arrow, or the instant you squeeze the trigger, the outcome rests upon your decision to shoot at that precise moment. If you make a poor judgment call and shot prematurely, or in some cases too late, the opportunity for a quick clean kill could end as promptly as your decision arrived to shoot.

If a deer hunter does not have a full understanding of the deer's anatomy, and is unsure how the animal should be positioned when he shoots, then he or she has little chance of avoiding a long tracking endeavor that may or may not lead to a recovery.

Consider that the deer is an excellent design of bone, muscle, and tissue, with the result a perfectly coordinated body which can undertake things we humans could never begin to endure. However, we have one advantage that the deer does not have - the ability to think and reason. We are the dominant species, so we are the hunters and the deer is the hunted.

Anyone who puts an effort into deer hunting wants to be successful, logically speaking. Hunters put many hours into pre-season scouting, and read biological research done on the deer, but it still boils down to one instant which decides success or failure. That moment of truth is "the shot."

Before the shot is taken, we have to know when and at what to shoot. Some beginning hunters are merely satisfied to shoot at the body, usually around the middle of the deer. This shot offers the most room for error, and leads to crippling. The bowhunter must pick a spot, just as the gun hunter who looks through the lens of a scope. This is when to know for sure what spot should be picked, and exactly where the spot is located.

When a deer hunter pulls the trigger or releases an arrow, it has to be with the intent to kill as quickly and humanely as possible. To accomplish this, it is important to know the vital organs that offer the quickest kill. The hunter should learn the whereabouts of all internal organs, both vital and non-vital, and know what organs offer the largest and quickest killing target. Additionally, he must know what organs are considered vital or non-vital. I will discuss these organs in this chapter, and again in later chapters where various wounds are mentioned.

The lungs, heart, and kidneys offer the quickest killing shots. Realistically, the kidneys make a poor target since they measure only about three and one-half inches long and two and one-half inches wide.

This leaves the lungs and heart as the prime targets. Even better, they are located closely together inside the chest cavity. The adult deer's inflated lungs are about nine inches long and six inches wide. The inflated lungs of a deer have often been compared to the size of a football.

Any shot through the front shoulders or up to four inches behind the shoulder will surely hit the lungs, providing the shot is not too far forward or too high. Later in this book you will read about the "black hole," an area of empty space near the lungs that often leads the hunter into a dreaded tracking situation.

The adult deer heart measures about five inches by four inches and is the shape of a grapefruit. Many hunters think of the heart as the deadliest organ and that they should aim for it. However, this is not the case. While it may be true that some heart shots will lead to a quick death, some do not.

Later you will read about a few heart-shot deer that did not succumb quickly. You should also consider the location of the heart when shooting. It lies low in the chest cavity, just above the front legs. Since it is a smaller target and requires a lower aiming point, there is a greater risk of missing your target. The lungs, on the other hand, enable a hunter to aim on center of the deer's body width and, of course, stay forward toward the shoulder. This allows more room for error and still obtains a vital hit.

The liver, just behind the chest diaphragm, is also close to the vital lungs. Many times a hunter aiming for the lungs will hit too far back and puncture the liver instead. Unfortunately, even though a liver hit will kill, it is not as vital an organ as the lungs. A liver-shot deer may not succumb for an hour or more, and will lead to a tedious tracking situation.

A wound in the paunch, which consists of the stomach and intestines, will also result in a dead deer. Nonetheless, a paunch wound leads to the same hazards as the liver hit. Tracking the animal is difficult, and it may take hours before a recovery is made. Any hunter who does not pick a spot forward in the deer and considers shooting for the middle of the animal should realize these consequences.

The major arteries will cause profuse bleeding and put a deer down in seconds. However, since they only have a diameter of about one-half inch, they offer the hunter no shot. When an artery is severed, it is usually by luck alone. I will own up to a few artery wounds, but will also say that all were appreciated.

We must look at shot placement from two aspects. The bowhunter's shot placement is a more limited area than that of the gun hunter. Make no mistake; a razor-sharp broadhead can kill as quickly as a bullet in most situations. I'm a two-season advocate, hunting with bow and gun each year. I have managed many times to see the different methods of destruction that the broadhead and bullet can do.

The broadhead, providing it is razor sharp, will slice and cut through anything so long as enough power is backing it and it doesn't hit bone. Even if it does hit bone, it may still penetrate completely. The broadhead causes severe hemorrhaging while the bullet literally crushes, destructs, and mutilates everything in its path. The shocking power of a bullet is enough in itself to do great damage. But that's not to say that any projectile will kill a deer no matter where it hits. On the contrary, many deer shot with bullets receive only superficial wounds. Just as a broadhead must hit vitals, so must a projectile.

There have been times when I had my bow in hand, only to wish it were my favorite deer gun, when a deer offered no shot at all for my bow. There have also been times when I would have gladly traded a bullet wound for an arrow hit. Regardless, you have to know how to make the best of the situation, when the time comes. The most critical time on a hunt is when you decide to shoot or not shoot. This means knowing your capabilities.

The gun hunter has to know his firearm and know it well; he or she has to know its limitations as far as distance and trajectory are concerned. The bowhunter must also know his equipment and his limitations. Some archers may take shots at distances of forty yards or more just because they are offered, even though their effective and accurate shooting range may be only twenty yards. Normally, most of my bow shots occur in the fifteen- to twenty-yard range. I have taken longer shots, but only when the animal was standing and positioned so that I knew my arrow could reach the vitals. Knowing my limitations prevents me from making a serious mistake. I've made some mistakes, sure, but seldom have they been the result of making a poor judgment and shooting when I shouldn't have.

The bowhunter must learn to control temptation on questionable shots. In fact, I believe most animals are poorly hit because a hunter took a shot he shouldn't have. That statement applies to both bow and gun hunters.

Another problem the archer faces is shooting at unknown distances. A deer does not walk around with a white aiming patch on its side, announcing the yardage from hunter to deer. I have seen bowhunters who can group arrows all day long at fifty yards, miss deer standing broadside at fifteen yards. As most archers know, shooting targets differs from shooting deer.

Different Shots

First, we will look at the quartering-into shot. This is a poor ground shot and an extremely poor tree-stand shot. It is a shot the bowhunter should forfeit. The only aiming point is the shoulder, a tough entry for any arrow, even with heavy poundage. The angle is totally wrong and causes the arrow to veer away from the vitals instead of toward them.

When hunting with a gun, I will take the quartering-into shot only if the deer is close and it seems improbable that it will turn broadside. If a deer is approaching my stand position, I will wait for a better opportunity,providing it does not become aware of my presence.

A deer facing into you is also be risky business unless the animal is extremely close. A bow shot should not be attempted on the ground or from an elevated stand position unless the deer is close and you are confident in your shooting ability at that distance. The gun hunter will have a better shooting opportunity at a greater distance, but even then the projectile must be carefully centered.

Some hunters are tempted to take the facing-into shot when an incoming deer suddenly realizes that danger may be ahead and decides to put on the brakes. After a little foot stomping and staring in the direction ahead, the deer finally shakes its head from side to side, trying to figure out what's going on. Temptation builds as the hunter realizes he will probably get no other shot. The truth is, most of the time we should forget about shooting. There is always a chance the deer may turn and offer a more promising shot.

I have always had mixed emotions about the effectiveness of the facing-away shot, and many hunters say it should be avoided. On the other hand, there are many experienced hunters who will take this shot, hunting with bow or gun, and there are times when it can be quite deadly, particularly at close range. I have seen arrow shots that were driven up the anal opening and completely destroyed everything all the way to the chest cavity. Just as important, when the heavy muscle area of the hip is damaged, it can put a deer in a big heap of trouble. But then again, there are times when a hip shot should not be taken. A later chapter discusses muscular wounds and what can be expected when a hip shot occurs.

The broadside shot is nearly perfect and offers easy access to the lungs for the bow and gun hunter. There are only two stipulations. One is that you have to be sure not to hit too far back, as the bullet or broadhead must stay forward in order to hit the vitals. The other objective is to be sure the front leg is forward. If the leg is back, the shoulder guards more of the lung area. Bowhunters will find this more of a problem than gun hunters will. The shoulder blade, hit in the right place, can sometimes stop an arrow in its tracks, preventing further penetration.

If the bowhunter is shooting from a tree stand, the shoulder blade becomes even more of a factor, and it becomes critical to hit the deer behind instead of on the shoulder. Close range here is a major factor. The closer the deer is to your stand position, the less area you have to shoot. Whenever I am in a tree, I would much rather have a deer standing fifteen yards away as opposed to five yards. The closer the deer is to you, the better the chance of hitting the animal high. Although the arrow is angling downward toward the lungs, there is always a chance that it may not get that far. A deer seems to get tougher the higher up on the back you hit.

I will always take the broadside shot whenever it is offered, regardless of whether I'm hunting with bow or gun. It just seems to be the kind of a shot you've hoped and waited for.

No one can argue against the angling-away shot as the perfect shot, and I would gladly trade ten quartering-into opportunities for one quartering away. The reason is simple. There are two places a bullet or broadhead could enter and still head all the way downtown.

The angling-away shot offers more margin for error than any other shot. You can enter just behind the shoulder and hit the vital lungs, or hit a few inches in front of the hip and still angle toward the primary organs. The latter entry would even hit the liver en route to the chest cavity.

When taken from a tree stand, the angling-away shot, may not be quite as easy as the ground shot. Once again, when shooting from an elevation, you have to hit slightly lower to be sure you are under the spine.

One final word about shooting a deer quartering away. If the animal is sharply quartering away, it is much more difficult to place your projectile or broadhead in a location that will reach the vital organs. If you hit too far forward, you could end up with a one-lung-shot deer to track. If you hit too far back, you could find yourself hitting the paunch only. The perfect quartering-away deer is one that is halfway between broadside and facing away.

Moving Deer

I don't believe any hunter should shy away from shooting at a walking deer, even when hunting with bow and arrow. You just have to use common sense and allow for the movement. As a deer progresses, its front leg is committed to go forward. If you time yourself to release the arrow when the leg comes back, the arrow will probably hit the animal when the leg is forward. Another advantage to a walking deer is the noise that it makes moving, which can be used to your benefit when drawing the bow or moving into position to draw.

I have never been an advocate of taking shots at running deer with gun or bow. I never attempt this shot when bowhunting unless the deer is extremely close and not traveling at excessive speed. The main thing a hunter has to do is practice timing his release. Although some archery clubs do offer practice sessions at moving targets, most of us do not practice releasing an arrow on moving targets.

The point is, why take risky, unwarranted shots? It might be fun to practice shooting at a moving target at a local club with your buddies, but when it comes to shooting at a running deer, you can usually count on not hitting the animal in the right place. Long shots are difficult on a standing deer, much less a running one. For most of us, it takes the best of our ability to make certain that even a close-range shot counts.

Something many bowhunters tend to overlook is how height affects the angle of entry. I primarily hunt from tree stands, whether I'm using bow or gun. There is not much disadvantage in the height angle affecting the gun hunter, but it can certainly affect the shot angle for the archer.

I once tested my shot angle by climbing to a height of fifteen feet and shooting an arrow at a particular target. Then I climbed to a height of twenty-two feet and shot another arrow at the same target. The different angle made for entirely different shots. Simply, the higher you climb, the less target you will have to shoot at. The shot taken from extremely high perches can easily cause you to miss, especial-ly if the deer is close to your stand. In fact, a sharp angle is much more likely to occur if the deer is only ten yards from your tree as opposed to one that is twenty yards. My preferred height when bowhunting is about eighteen feet. M a n y years ago, I got by with hunting lower, but times have changed and the deer have become more educated. In fact, I sometimes climb higher if I'm in an area where the deer have been pressured. Even if the deer look up, my greater height gives me a distinct advantage. Hunters should climb to their comfortable level, however, since hunting uncomfortably can spoil a shooting opportunity.

Although shot placement is important, it really boils down to your own ability. You must know what you are or are not capable of doing. Anyone who doesn't practice this policy and takes shots beyond his capability will continue to miss and wound deer.

Many hunters don't realize they have made a bad shooting decision until it is too late. I have wounded my share of deer and made mistakes along the way. But I have learned from those mistakes, to the point where I'm confident I can make a clean and humane kill whenever I pull the trigger or release an arrow. Getting to that level should be every hunter's goal.

There is much more to tracking than following a blood trail. An experienced tracker looks for blood smears, tissue and beds, and he knows if the wounded deer is walking or running.

Chapter 5

Blood Trails and Tracking

The best trackers are those who are patient. Following the trail of a wounded deer effectively requires you to do so slowly, cautiously, and quietly. You must consider many factors before starting to blood trail. This chapter will focus on tracking techniques, beginning with the precise location of where the deer was shot. Following a blood trail can be simple, or it can be difficult. Sometimes we make it more difficult than it is, while other times it is much more difficult than we expected. The location of the wound, the type of terrain, and how soon you begin tracking will all play essential roles in trailing the deer.

How long should you wait before tracking a wounded deer? Each hunter should make his decision based on the wound.

Tracking a wounded deer is an art that some have mastered through experience. Others jump right in and do a fine job the first time out. Good trackers do much more than follow drops of blood on the ground, however. A skilled tracker knows to look for blood smears, tissue, and hair. He knows if a wounded deer has bedded, is walking or running, and he can often follow a trail when blood does not even exist. Most important, he does not assume anything.

Before going on, let me say that there is one fact that stands out above the rest. A large amount of external blood does not necessarily mean that a deer is going down. Many of us have experienced these types of blood trails, but they do not always lead to a downed deer. I have seen some superficial muscle wounds bleed extensively for long distances. On the other hand, I have seen wounded deer go down within 100 yards, without leaving one drop of blood on the ground.

First Blood

There are many reasons why you might find blood at the location the deer stood when you took the shot. There are also many reasons why you might not find blood until you have gone a considerable distance from where the deer was standing. Moreover, there are also reasons why a deer may not bleed at all. The location of the wound, angle of the shot, diameter of the entry and departure hole, penetration of the projectile or arrow, and height of the entry and departure hole will decide how quickly a deer bleeds externally.

Extremely low wounds sometimes result in blood getting to the ground immediately, whereas high wounds will seldom result in blood getting to the ground until the deer has run a fair distance. Such was the case when southern Indiana bowhunter Ed Rinehart shot a small buck only a few yards from the base of his tree. The arrow entered high and just behind the shoulder, but did not exit. We spent more than an hour looking for blood of this lung-shot deer, but could not find anything. We finally found the buck piled up 125 yards from where Ed shot it. This deer did not leave one drop of external blood.

My dad once shot a buck from a tree stand, hitting it low in the stomach. Blood was splattered everywhere at the precise location where the deer stood. However, the blood slacked off to pin drops only fifty yards from that spot. After tracking the buck another twenty-five yards, the blood stopped. We later recovered the deer and discovered that the arrow had entered the deer in the bottom of its paunch, and exited in the middle of its underbelly.

I used these examples to give you an idea of why you do or do not find blood quickly. As mentioned previously, every wound will vary. Despite these variations, I will always look for blood at the location where the deer stood when shot. If I don't find blood, I will do my best to locate hair and scuffed marks. Then I will widen the search and attempt to find the first blood. In the following chapters, you will read about each type of wound imaginable, and how soon you can expect to find blood. Most tracking endeavors cannot begin until you find the first blood. After finding the first blood, you can examine its color and know when to begin tracking.

Colors of Blood

Blood is not just red. It can be bright or dark. It can be darker than dark, or crimson instead of bright. Each wound gives off a certain color of blood, and that color should guide you when deciding how soon you should track the deer.

For instance, dark blood is the result of an abdomen wound. Muscle wounds result in bright blood, similar to lung-shot deer. However, a lung-shot deer may produce blood that appears almost pink. Heart, some artery, and kidney wounds usually result in bright to crimson blood.

If the hunter does not pay special attention to the color of blood, he may not know how long to wait before he begins to track the animal. The bowhunter, if he or she retrieves the arrow, can often determine the color of blood by looking at the shaft. If the shaft cannot be located, the bowhunter must do the same as the firearm hunter and locate the first few drops to make a determination. However, always consider the angle of the deer and the path of the projectile or arrow shaft. It is possible for a deer to leave both bright and dark blood. For instance, if your arrow or bullet enters the deer near its hip and exits through the paunch, it is possible you could find bright and dark blood. In this case the bright blood is usually more prevalent, but the fact remains that both colors could exist. If a hunter shoots a deer quartering toward him, his broadhead or projectile may enter the animal just behind the shoulder and exit in front of the hip. He will also find bright and dark blood. The bright blood would be from the wound to one lung, and the dark blood would be the result of the wound to the stomach and/or intestines.

Complete arrow or projectile penetration may determine how quickly you find blood. In case you're wondering, two holes are always better than one. First, consider that the path of the arrow or projectile is longer than it would be if it did not exit. The more it penetrates, the better the chance it will hit a vital organ, or artery. Additionally, an exit hole increases the chance of external blood getting to the ground, and the possibility that you will find blood sooner than you would have if only an entry hole existed.

Examining Arrows

Bowhunters can often obtain facts from a spent arrow, facts that can aid them in tracking. First, let's look at penetration.

Some trackers believe that good things come from an arrow that remains in the deer. For instance, it could keep the entry and/or departure hole from clotting. There is probably some truth to this theory, since coagulation can occur. I would much rather see a pass-through, though, simply because I will probably locate the arrow, and there will be a better chance the broadhead has hit vitals.

If tallow is present on an arrow, it indicates certain wounds. These wounds will be discussed in later chapters. However, many wounds where tallow is found do not result in easy-to-follow blood trails, or dead deer. Exceptions do exist, however.

You may determine a pass-through by the straightness of the arrow shaft, and the blood you find between the nock and the broadhead. Bent or broken arrows, even when found at the location the deer stood when shot, sometimes indicate the arrow did not pass through. When the arrow hits, the deer often lunges. If the arrow hits a tree or heavy brush, it may break off or bend. You can usually determine pen-etration by how far the blood comes up the shaft, and by the location of the bend or break. If the arrow is bent or broken on the front half (nock end), you probably did not penetrate totally.

On the other hand, if the bend or brake is on the business end, the arrow has probably penetrated totally. You may also find blood on just one side of the arrow. This may indicate a graze, but not always. Debris and foliage, particularly when wet, can clean an arrow on one side, or all sides. An arrow that is found after you track a deer for a given distance also tells a story. For instance, an arrow that has penetrated totally will usually come out broadhead first, and fall to the ground from the exit hole. This is true whether you shot the deer from a tree stand or the ground. It will not work its way out through the entry hole if it has penetrated totally.

Sometimes, if a deer carries the arrow, it will bump into debris or trees, causing it to break apart and flip away from the blood trail. I can't tell you how many times I have tracked and found a deer, yet failed to see the arrow along the blood trail. Backtracking will usually turn up the arrow, however.

Waiting Before Tracking

How long should you wait before tracking a wounded deer? Will waiting increase your chances of finding the animal, or will the delay hinder you? These questions are always sources of debate among hunters. Some hunters say you should push every deer, while others say it's best to go after some deer right away. A few believe you should delay tracking any wounded deer immediately. I will give you my opinions, and in doing so, explain how I have come to these conclusions. Although research has played a part in my opinions, my primary beliefs have come from in-the-field experiences.

When I started deer hunting in the 1960s, hunters always thought it best to sit back and wait twenty or thirty minutes before picking up the trail of a wounded deer. It was believed that the deer would bed down, stiffen, and eventually die if left alone, or be stiff enough so that it couldn't get out of its bed. If you jumped the deer, and it obviously had not stiffened enough to lay there and give you another shot, you should have waited longer before you started tracking.

Today, we know that a wound does not cause a deer to stiffen and die. It is the severity of the wound that will cause the animal to succumb, coupled with the length of time you wait before tracking it.

Rigor mortis is the stiffening of muscles after death. After a deer dies, it will begin stiffening. Various muscles will stiffen first, after a given length of time, although variables may affect the results.

John D. Gill of the Maine Department of Inland Fisheries, and David C. O'Meara, of Maine's Department of Animal Pathology, conducted a survey in the 1960s to estimate the time of death in white-tailed deer. For several days, they observed the carcasses of eighty-five deer shot by hunters. The two gathered data on body temperature, eye appearance, pupil diameter, and muscle stiffness. Their article and findings appeared in the Journal Of Wildlife Management, Volume 29, No. 3, July 1965.

To check rigor mortis, Gill and O'Meara gently flexed various joints by grasping the outer edge of the jaw, the upper end of the neck, the forelimb above and below either the wrist (corpus) or the elbow (humerus), the hind leg above and below either the ankle (tarsus), or the knee (femur). The team made certain they did not reduce or break rigor, and the degree of stiffness present was recorded as "None", "one-quarter inch", "one-half inch", "three-quarter inch", or "complete".

				Hours since Death			
Rigor Mortis		1	2	3	4	5	6
Jaw	None	0					
	Partial	6	6				
	Stiff	1	18	28	24	14	18
Neck	None	4	14	6	1		
	Partial		2	16	28	14	20
	Stiff		1	4	10	13	17
Wrist (Carpus)	None	7	23	15	8	2	2
	Partial		5	24	37	33	26
	Stiff			1	5	4	15
Elbow (humerus)	None	7	10				
	Partial		12	20	12	10	5
	Stiff		3	20	38	29	49
Ankle (Tarsus)	None	4	3	1			
	Partial	1	12	14	11	8	3
	Stiff		2	12	16	16	18
Knee (femur)	None	4	2				
	Partial	1	12	5	3	1	2
	Stiff		3	20	21	18	20

Rigor Mortis Table: Numbers of observations of rigor mortis in deer. (Journal of Wildlife Management July 1965, John D. Gill and David O'Meara).

It was observed that muscles gradually stiffened soon after death, but would later relax because of internal chemical changes. Temperatures and other factors contributed to the rate of change in various parts of the body. Although more stiffening occurred in this sequence - jaw, knee, elbow, ankle, neck, and wrist, exceptions were mostly due to these four reasons:

1. Wounds may prevent, weaken, or delay rigor near tissue damage.
2. Rough handling may reduce or eliminate stiffening.
3. Differences due to air temperature (possibly masked by other variables).
4. Freezing confused with rigor mortis.

It was noted that jaws stiffened within two hours. Gill and O'Meara claimed the lower jaw clamped tightly with the lips concealing the teeth, although the tongue protruded. As the jaw relaxed, the front teeth became visible and the outer end of the jaw would flex about inch.

Stiffness, of course, may help you determine how long a deer has been dead, but it is not a factor before death. However, there is another consideration when wondering how long to wait before tracking a wounded deer.

We know that a running whitetail has about three times the heart rate per minute of a bedded deer. Thus, it is safe to assume that a moving deer will bleed more than a bedded deer, whether the bleeding is internal or external. Does this mean that a wounded deer should be tracked right away?

I say no, even though these facts have led some to believe that we should push all wounded deer, regardless of the location of the wound. Some hunters claim that a moving deer will bleed out and die sooner than one that is bedded. Personally, I believe we should throw this theory out the door along with the stiffening hypothesi.

I will agree that heart rate and bleeding increases with movement. However, keep in mind that a moving deer is getting farther away with each step. I've had times when it took me an hour to follow a deer for 100 yards or less, simply because blood did not get to the ground when the deer was walking. And that's the bottom line: A wound that allows blood to get to the ground, particularly muscle wounds, could call for immediate tracking. On the other hand, a gut-shot deer that may leave very few drops of blood, or no blood at all on the ground for a long distance, should never be tracked immediately. Consider that stomach and intestinal matter may clog a hole in a deer, preventing blood from getting to the ground. A large broadhead or projectile may make a big hole, but that doesn't necessarily mean that an entry or departure hole will remain open and allow blood to reach the ground. I also know that a gut-shot deer will not succumb quickly, and will usually bed down if not pushed.

When tracking a deer, it is primarily a blood trail that will lead you to the animal. Obviously, the tracking becomes more difficult if no blood is present. Now consider the distance a deer may travel. In the case of stomach and intestinal wounds, many deer lay up a short distance from where they were shot. These wounds are fatal, and deer with such wounds will die within a given number of hours depending upon precise location of the wound - organ and artery damage. However, if you push the animal to increase the heart rate and induce bleeding, you still may get no more blood on the ground than you would have if you left the deer alone. Meanwhile, the deer gets farther away, and the chances of recovering it grow slimmer. Consider slowly pushing a deer for five minutes, and how far it could travel. If you allow the gut-shot deer to stay bedded, it will still bleed internally - perhaps slower than it would have if moving, but nonetheless the end result is still death. The best advice I can give is to consider distance. The further you must track a deer, the less chance you have of a recovery.

Fortunately, many hunters do wait to track stomach and intestinal-shot deer. But some insist upon waiting to track any deer, including those with muscle wounds, where increased bleeding could lead the animal to succumb when it otherwise may not have. Thus, you should evaluate every wound when deciding how long to wait. For instance, why wait to track a double lung-shot deer that will probably go down in seconds, a short distance away? Then again, waiting a few minutes and sizing up the situation won't hurt anything since the animal will obviously not be going anywhere. Waiting too long to track a deer with a muscle wound, though, could be damaging when coagulation begins.

I have provided a table that you can use as a guide. I have stuck to this waiting schedule, as have other veteran deer hunters I know. The results have been spectacular and have led to the recovery of more than a few deer. Of course, you must know the location of the wound, and be aware of how it will affect tracking. Other factors, such as too many hunters in the area, terrain, weather, and darkness may also affect the length of time you should wait to track a deer. In the following chapters, I have supplied anecdotes, and information about specific types of wounds that tell why it is best to wait or delay tracking.

Lack of patience should never tempt you to begin tracking a deer immediately. When I shoot a deer, I'm as eager as the next guy to get after it and see my trophy up close. However, you must be patient and wait if necessary. I would that many hunters who pursue an animal right away do so because they just couldn't stand the agony of waiting. Just as harmful would be waiting, but not waiting long enough. For instance, if you should wait for four hours and you wait for only one hour to track a stomach-shot deer, you will probably push the deer farther away, just as you would have done if you had started tracking at once.

Location of Wound	Time to Wait Before Tracking
Artery (major)	20 minutes
Heart	20 minutes
Hip (muscle only)	20 minutes
Intestines	8 – 12 hours
Kidneys	20 minutes
Leg	20 minutes
Liver	2 to 3 hours
Lungs	20 minutes
Neck (muscle only)	20 minutes
Shoulder (muscle only)	20 minutes
Spine or Neck Vertebrate	0
Stomach	4 – 6 hours

Time to Wait Table: The author's schedule for waiting to track a wounded deer, by wound location. Variables may exist that will prompt or delay time to wait.

Throughout this book, I suggest that some wounds call for immediate tracking. After viewing the table, you might wonder why these wounds suggest you wait twenty minutes. Actually, staying put for a few minutes after shooting an animal will help you gain composure, and recall a few events that may help to put you on the blood trail. You may not pick up the trail until twenty minutes after the shot, but you are still in immediate pursuit and will probably prevent coagulation.

When you do pursue a deer right away, you must move slowly and quietly from one drop of blood to another. Avoid getting ahead of yourself if you lose the blood trail, and keep a constant look ahead for a bedded or moving deer.

Reading Tracks

Just finding tracks when you trail a deer is helpful, but being able to read those tracks will provide valuable tracking insight. Tracks show you if a deer is running or walking. Tracks may indicate other factors, including the sex of the deer, size, and sometimes the type of wound the animal encountered.

Various types of wounds will cause a deer to run differently than it might have otherwise. For instance, a heart-shot deer often runs much more erratically than a lung-shot deer does. The running tracks of a deer with a stomach wound are totally different from one with a hip wound. Joseph Bruner, a German tracker, studied eight different sets of tracks of wounded deer. In 1909, Bruner provided an illustration of the track patterns in a book titled Tracks And Tracking (see table). In recent years, I have attempted to determine the accuracy of the track patterns and wounds depicted in the table. In many cases, the tracks I followed did not stay visible long enough, the deer stayed in woods and thickets and did not produce tracks, or the animal dropped dead before I could evaluate the tracks. Although I have yet to compare precisely the tracks recorded by Bruner and deer I have trailed, I have seen similarities - primarily the track patterns as a result of wounds to the foreleg and hind leg.

The back hooves of a deer are slightly smaller than the front hooves. It is difficult to provide measurements, since the size of the track is dependent upon the subspecies of the deer, age, and size. However, most adult whitetail tracks will be two and one-half to three inches in length when the animal walks. When running, the length and width of the tracks are slightly larger.

When you follow the tracks of a wounded deer, they often lead into other tracks, leaving you confused. This can happen in snow, even when it appears for a moment that you could follow the animal to the end of the continent. When the tracks you follow merge with other tracks, it is best to bend over, get close to the ground, and proceed cautiously. One thing you can bet on is that most wounded deer do not attempt to travel with others unless the wound is minor, such as a scrape under the brisket, or a nick on the leg. I've also noticed that severely wounded young deer do not attempt to get back with the doe, nor does a severely wounded doe try to find her fawn.

A	B	C	D	E	F	G	H

Wounded Deer Walking Patterns: (A) Trail of a deer shot through brisket with leg broken low in shoulder. (B) Trail of a deer shot high through the shoulders. (C) Trail of a deer with a broken foreleg - the lower the leg is broken, the more pronounced the drage mark. (D) Trail of a deer wit a broken hind leg - the lower the leg is broken, the more pronounced the drag mark. (E) Trail of a deer shot through the ham. (F) This trail usually means that the animal was shot through the intestines, liver or lungs. (G) Same as F but did not penetrate to the lungs. (H) The cross jump results from a bullet through the intestines or liver with the animal standing broadside to the hunter. (Joseph Bruner, *Tracks And Tracking).*

Whenever I shoot a deer that is with others, it may run away with them, but will not stay with them long. After a short sprint, the wounded animal usually separates from the others. Thus, if you can't find blood near the location where you hit a deer, follow all the tracks but pay special attention to a track that suddenly separates from the others, or a track pattern that differs from the others.

When tracking a deer, it also helps to know if a deer is running or walking. For example, if walking tracks suddenly change to running tracks, it could be the deer detected your presence. Alternatively, the deer may have been bedded and detected your approach. Whenever a walking deer suddenly runs, I evaluate the situation carefully. I may stay on the trail, or I may sit down and wait.

There are two ways to tell if a deer is walking - by tracks and by blood. First, we'll discuss tracks.

A running deer brings its back feet ahead of the front feet. The tracks will appear as a set of four tracks, with the tracks of the back feet parallel with each other, and in front of the tracks made by the front feet. Each set of four tracks will be spaced two and one-half to three feet apart.

LARRY SMAIL

A running deer brings its back feet ahead of the front feet. Instead of evenly spaced tracks, you will find set of four tracks each.

When a deer walks, you will find two straight lines of tracks about fourteen to twenty inches apart. That's understandable, if you consider the body width of a deer. The toes of the tracks will also be turned outward slightly. The straight-line appearance of the tracks can differ, as well as the outward angle of the toes when certain conditions exist. For instance, when a doe's udder is filled with milk, the tracks made by the back hooves may be farther apart than the tracks made by the front hooves, and the tracks of the back hooves may curve more outward than the front ones. It is also believed that track patterns of does in estrous, and bucks in rut change slightly. A certain wound may also have an affect on how the tracks appear.

For many years, veteran hunters and trackers have argued about determining the sex of the deer by its tracks. The debate will continue, as some tracks may allow you to determine the sex of the deer, while others will leave you scratching your head.

The size of the track may help, but only when it comes from a big buck, and you are familiar with the size of the tracks of an average adult deer in your area. If you have seen hundreds of tracks in the area made by deer weighing 125 to 150 pounds, and then come across the tracks of a 200-pound deer, you will probably see a noticeable difference, and believe they are that of a buck. However, I have seen one and one-half-year-old, 150-pound bucks with tracks as large as two-and-one-half-year-old, 200-pound bucks. In addition, tracks may appear larger and deeper in snow and soft soil than they would on a dry, dirt surface. And since a running deer's track appears larger than a walking deer's track, it wouldn't be wise to estimate the sex or size of the deer if it is running.

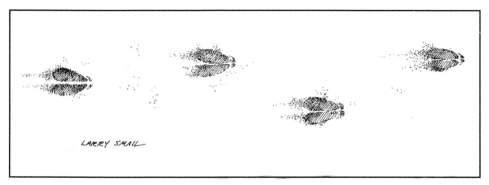

LARRY SMAIL

A walking deer's tracks will be in two straight lines, those made by the left, and those made by the right hooves.

You will often find drag marks in snow when you follow the tracks of a buck, providing the snow is a certain depth. A buck seems to walk more clumsily than a doe, and it's a fact that does raise their hooves slightly higher than a buck's, probably because their pelvic structure differs from bucks. In deep snow, all deer leave drag marks. In fact, when examining the tracks of deer in captivity, I've found that the only way to see drag marks of bucks is when the snow is one to three inches deep.

In heavy leaves, you may also determine drag marks. However, that is very difficult to do since the depth of leaves and terrain can vary every few yards. The best chance of seeing a buck's drag marks in leaves is when the terrain is level, most of the leaves have fallen and are dry, and there has not been heavy deer traffic through that specific area.

A deer's hooves are designed to provide traction, but not on slick surfaces. On ice, a deer walks very carefully, and appears to know that its hooves could slide out from under him. If the animal goes down, it may not be able to get back up.

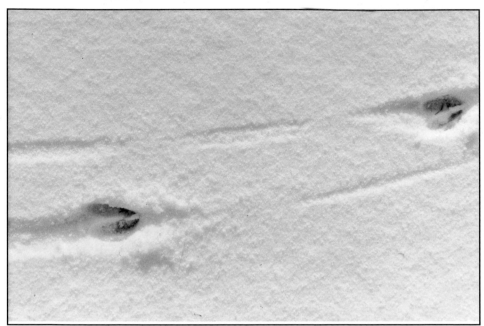

Bucks will leave drag marks behind their tracks when they walk in snow. However, if the snow gets deep, all deer will leave drag marks.

Blood Trailing

Tracking a wounded deer, particularly one that does not leave an easy-to-follow blood trail, requires skill. Most hunters, who have mastered the art of tracking, did so because of experience. However, help is advantageous, regardless of your abilities.

I always find myself much more nervous when tracking my own deer. Secondly, it really helps to have more eyes looking for blood and a downed deer. My son and I have shared many tracking experiences in the past two decades, and I am always glad to have his help. He is a patient tracker, as are many of my friends who are proficient trackers. In recent years my wife, Vikki, has also assisted me with trailing, and while she usually stands patiently on the last drop of blood, she often finds more blood in that location while I'm out ahead somewhere.

Just how many should be involved when the tracking begins? I prefer a party of two or three. Four hunters are pushing it. I have often assisted when the tracking party consisted of four, five, or more. I find things too noisy and careless, which can lead to a trampled blood trail or a spooked deer. When three people track the deer, one can stay on the last blood while four eyes continue looking for the next drop.

Although some blood trails are easy to see and can be followed rapidly, most difficult trailing episodes go from drop to drop. When you find one drop, look closely for another without moving too far ahead. If you can't find another drop within sight of the last, mark the spot before getting too far away. Never get in a hurry and start looking for a downed deer too quickly. Some hunters would rather look for a deer than a drop of blood. Their eyes never focus on the ground and surrounding debris for sign. This leads to careless tracking, and may spoil a recovery opportunity.

Walk to the sides of a blood trail as you follow it. If you walk over the blood, you'll kick up any drops that you've already found. While this may be okay if you find the deer a short distance ahead, it certainly won't do you any good if you have to return to the blood drops later on. For instance, what if the deer you're following suddenly begins backtracking? Surprisingly, some deer do turn around and go back in the same direction they just came from. If you walk a couple of feet to the sides of the blood trail, and mark it consistently, you should have no problem returning to the original trail if the deer turns around and walks back from where it came.

As mentioned previously, it helps to tie white tissue paper or trail-marking ribbon a few feet above the ground each time you find blood. Don't lay your marker on the ground, or tie it a foot or two above the ground, since it would be hard to see from a short distance away.

It may not be necessary to mark the trail if you are finding large amounts of blood, but it is necessary whenever you find blood droplets several feet apart. The markers allow you to return to the last blood, and they allow you to see the directional travel of the deer you are trailing. Many times, after losing a blood trail, I have looked back through the woods to see 100 yards or more of markers. I can then notice if the deer is veering right or left, and can concentrate on looking for blood in another direction. When the tracking ends, return to your location and remove the markers. Tissue paper will decompose eventually, but this may take several weeks. Seeing tissue paper strung through woods is not a pretty sight, and it won't do much for your hunting area.

Speaking of hunting areas, be aware that a major tracking episode will probably hurt your hunting area for several days. Consistently, I have seen areas dry up immediately following a trailing endeavor. However, when you consider the disturbance and the human scent left in the area, it's no wonder the hunting becomes stale. I always hope for a good rain to wash out human scent as soon as the tracking ends.

I've said this before: Despite what you may have heard, the volume of blood you find on the ground has little to do with your chances of recovering a deer. I have heard hunters (myself included) say, "This deer is about to go down." These opinions are often based on a heavy blood trail. However, many scrape and muscle wounds cause excessive bleeding that do not always result in a downed deer. These wounds produce blood trails that would make you believe an artery was severed, but after a couple of hundred yards or less, they begin to tell a different story. On the other hand, many stomach and intestinal-shot deer leave little or no blood, but will result in a downed deer. For this reason, it is best not to speculate when it comes to the amount of external blood, since it could affect your persistence to continue tracking if the going gets tough.

The amount of blood that gets to the ground often depends upon the location of the wound. Don't be mislead if you find very little blood. Many deer that do not bleed much externally may still be mortally wounded.

Large cuts across the bottom of the deer may result in excessive bleeding when the broadhead or projectile does not penetrate into the body cavity. They simply make a long incision. You might determine this type of wound at the location the deer stood when you shot. A large section of hair, sometimes up to several inches, will be found on the ground after grazing an animal.

When the blood trail becomes difficult to follow, get down on your knees, or bend down to look for blood. You'll be surprised how much more blood you can find when your eyes are only a foot above the ground, particularly when nickel-size droplets suddenly turn into drops the size of pinheads. Getting on all fours is probably better than bending, but it can also damage an existing blood trail.

Many blood trails intensify as you follow them, while others begin to weaken. Several factors will determine the amount of blood that gets to the ground as the deer moves farther away. For example, you may follow the trail of a running deer that received a muscle wound. Each time the deer's heart pumps hard, blood is expelled through an entry and/or exit hole. If this deer begins walking, the blood trail may weaken.

A low hit can also cause more blood to get to the ground early in the tracking than it will later. A high hit works the opposite, since the blood you find on the ground may intensify after the deer travels a short distance. Then, consider a low hit, and blood in the body cavity. As the deer travels, internal bleeding may occur. This blood soon reaches the hole in the deer and finds its way to the ground. Thus, the blood trail begins intensifying as the deer moves farther along the trail. Later,

I discuss specific wounds and what kind of blood trails will occur as a result of these wounds.

Get close to the ground if the blood trail becomes difficult to follow, but make certain you stay to the sides of the trail and don't walk over blood.

You may find two trails of blood instead of one when complete penetration occurs. The possibility of two blood trails depends upon the location of wound, and the height of your entry and exit holes. However, if a single blood trail suddenly turns into two, make certain the deer is not backtrailing.

Previously, I told how you can tell if a deer is running or walking by its tracks. You can also determine if a deer is standing, walking, or running by examining blood droplets. When a deer walks slowly, you will find a line of droplets. Each droplet is round and completely encircled by thin splatter marks. The shape of the droplets is the same as those made by a standing deer, except they are not in a line. Instead, you may find several droplets in one location, perhaps covering a one- or two-foot area. When a deer stands, you might find a pool of blood as each drop merges with another. The amount of blood you find on the ground depends upon the wound, and how long the deer stood there.

When a deer runs, the blood droplets are oblong. You may find splatter marks on the wide end of the oval droplet, but not on the opposite end. The wider portion of the droplet, which has the splatter marks, also indicates the direction the deer is traveling.

When you find blood in the deer's tracks, it usually indicates a leg, shoulder, neck, or ham wound. The blood ends up in the track after running down a leg, but this usually doesn't occur until the animal has traveled for a distance. It is also possible you may find blood on the ground between the left and right hooves, or about the center of the deer. This often occurs when you track a neck-shot deer, or if your departure hole came out on the bottom side of the deer.

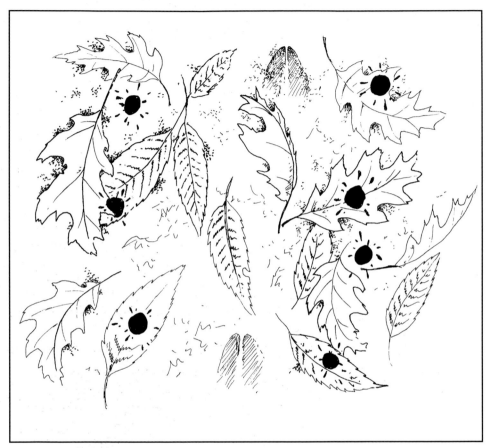

When you find two blood trails instead of one, it probably means the deer is bleeding out of both sides. However, always make certain the deer hasn't walked back the same trail it came through earlier.

Always examine the blood carefully to make certain it is indeed blood. There's nothing worse than losing a blood trail, then to have someone holler, "Blood," and then discover it isn't blood at all. The woods floor is full of red, maroon, and purple colors. I've seen some maple leaves that had red blotches on them that look exactly like blood. Many types of berries splatter on the ground and appear as blood. When you are uncertain, use your saliva to wet the spot you suspect is blood. If it doesn't wipe off, you know it isn't blood. Another thought is to use hydrogen peroxide or a commercial blood tester.

When blood dries, it becomes darker and is harder to see. The more blood there is in one location, the longer it will stay wet. However, if you follow a dry blood trail and it suddenly turns wet, you probably got close to the deer and sent it moving.

LARRY SMAIL

A deer that walks will leave blood droplets that are round with splatter marks surrounding the drops.

When a blood trail expires, I will begin looking for blood smears on rocks, trees, tall weeds, and other debris. If I don't find smears, I resort to following trails and looking for tracks. If tracks are not visible, I look for another means of trailing the deer. For instance, when a deer runs in leaves, it leaves an obvious trail. The leaves are kicked out and piled up near the locations where the deer's hooves come off the ground. Even if the deer walks in leaves, careful tracking may allow you to follow the trail. When the hooves of a walking deer come down, they curl the leaves under each hoof.

Finally, don't take things for granted when tracking a wounded deer. This can get you into trouble. I try to look at each trailing experience as a unique one. I often know what to expect, but avoid making guesses. I stay on a blood trail as long as possible, and then resort to tracking the animal the best I can when blood is not getting to the ground. When I can't track the deer any longer by blood or tracks, and all other efforts to locate them have been to no avail, I begin the recovery attempt. For this reason, it's important for you to read the chapter, "Last-Ditch Efforts."

When a deer runs, it leaves a different blood trail. Notice the oval shape of these blood droplets, and that splatter marks are only at one end of the droplet.

Many leaves and berries can resemble blood. If you have any doubt if what you found is blood, test it with hydrogen peroxide or a commercial blood tester.

The String Tracker

The bowhunter who chooses to use a string tracker may find it beneficial when it comes to recovering a deer. However, you should be aware of a few disadvantages.

A friend of mine, Woody Williams, used a string tracker in Ontario while hunting black bear. After shooting a bear, he nervously watched the string unwind until it stopped. He believed the bear was down.

Shortly after dark, Woody and I got on the trail of the wounded bear. We found blood here and there, but easily followed the line that had unraveled from the string tracker. About 150 yards later, we reached the end of the line (I mean that literally). It had caught in debris and broken. We never recovered the bear.

String tracking line is tough, but it can break. Archers should also be aware that arrow flight and accuracy can change when using a string tracker. The farther you shoot, the more drop you will have. When I used a string tracker for the first time several years ago, I found it necessary to adjust my sight when shooting at twenty yards. My arrows dropped about four inches. At thirty yards, the drop increased dramatically. If you plan to use a string tracker, plan to practice often.

Wind can also cause problems when using a string tracker. The loop of line that dangles loosely from the canister to the business end of the arrow may catch on accessories or limbs, causing the string to unravel.

On the positive side, a string tracker can give you several hundred yards of easy tracking if you make a bad hit. If the line gets to the end of the spool, sim-ply tie on line from an extra spool. This can add another few hundred yards of easy tracking. A string tracker may also help you track a deer if it rains. Finally, a string tracker makes it easy to locate your arrow when you miss, or if it totally penetrates. If the arrow does go all the way through the deer, however, you may find two trails of line when you follow it.

Tracking with Dogs

No hunter will dispute a dog's ability to follow a trail. We also know that a dog will do a better job than we can of tracking a wounded deer. After all, they can follow a trail by scent, while we must use our eyes.

However, the idea of using dogs does not appeal to every hunter. Instead, they believe that it is the hunter's responsibility to do everything humanly possible to recover the animal, without the aid of a dog.

This is a touchy subject, so I might as well jump in and give my opinion. I don't have a problem with using dogs in some tracking situations, but a thin line exists. Where dogs are legal, I often wonder if it can lead to careless shooting on a hunter's part. If they have access to a quality dog, would they take risky shots? Stress is another factor. Is it possible that an unleashed dog would cause undue stress when it trails a deer that has received only a minor wound? I believe so. If I started deer hunting in a state that allowed dogs to trail deer, I might see it from a different perspective. But I have another opinion. If a deer is doomed and will surely die, such as a gut-shot deer, and all tracking efforts by the hunter have failed, it would seem better to use a dog than to not find the animal at all.

At the time of this writing, trailing dogs are legal in fifteen states. In one of these states, however, dogs must be on a leash. There is also an organization ded-icated to helping others recover deer with the aid of dogs, but not until the hunter has made a thorough recovery attempt.

I must tip my hat to Deer Search, Inc. (D.S.I.), a New York group of vol-unteers that uses leashed dogs to track and find wounded deer. There are sixty members in the western chapter, where Mike Coppola is a trustee, and past presi-dent. According to Coppola, his chapter received about 550 requests to track wounded deer in 1999. He reported that the chapter assisted in about 200 of the requests. Each request is evaluated when the call comes in. Coppola said that a large percentage of the wounds are shoulder hits. However, D.S.I makes every effort to help hunters recover liver and gut-shot deer. Even the organization's brochure states, "D.S.I. is NOT a hunter's crutch, it is an agency of Last Resort. After you have tried everything else you know to do and still circumstances prevent you from recovering your wounded deer (or bear), call Deer Search, Inc. For more information, contact Deer Search, Inc., P.O. Box 853, Pleasant Valley, NY 12569, or call 716/648-4355.

States that Allow the Use of Trailing Dogs

Alabama	New York
Arkansas	North Carolina
California	South Carolina
Florida	South Dakota
Georgia	Texas
Louisiana	Virginia
Mississippi	Wisconsin*
Nebraska	

Dogs must be on a leash.

Tracking Accessories

Deer hunters pack along all kinds of gadgets, from grunt calls and scents to wind-checking devices. Why not prepare a tracking kit? Surprisingly, you can include about everything you could possibly need in a fanny pack or small daypack. If you are hunting close to home or a vehicle, you can leave the pack stored away until duty calls.

Tracking Kit Essentials

Compass	String Tracker
Field Dressing Gloves	Toilet Paper
Hydrogen Peroxide	Topographic Map
Knife	Tracking Book
Light / Lantern	Trail Marking Ribbon
Radio	

Store these items in a fanny pack or daypack, and keep them close by.

   The most important items are probably markers to place above blood droplets, a proper light for tracking in the dark, and hydrogen peroxide, or a commercial blood testing chemical. However, there is an array of other items listed in the Tracking Kit table that you may find useful. Some of the items you may have with you, but nonetheless the kit makes certain they will be there when tracking a deer. I would also suggest you pack along this book if space allows. This will make it possible for you to recognize the type of wound you are dealing with by blood color and hair. Additionally, you will have quick access to tracking tips.

   I consistently pack a tracking kit, hoping that some of the items won't be used. As they say, though, "It's better to have it and not need it than need it and not have it."

To make certain you have everything when tracking becomes necessary, consider packing a tracking kit in a daypack or fanny pack.

© **Ted Rose**

Taking time to evaluate all the signs and then planning a course of action is often crucial to locating a wounded deer.

Chapter 6

Tracking Factors

Following a blood trail and reading tracks are only part of tracking. Other factors to consider include weather, darkness, and terrain. You must also be aware of what a deer might do next. There is no way you can make accurate assumptions all the time, but the more you know about wounded deer-when they tend to bed, whether they're likely to go uphill or down, when they might circle-the better tracker you will become.

When Deer Bed Down

You may follow a blood trail through open hardwoods or other areas, only to have it go into a dense area. This often occurs when the deer is about to bed down. Just how far the deer goes into a dense area before it beds depends upon the severity of the wound, and whether the deer has detected the trackers. I have found that most deer lay up almost immediately after entering a thicket. I have also found that certain types of dense areas are more likely to attract wounded deer.

If a wounded deer suddenly turns into a thick area, it will probably bed down. If the deer is not aware of the tracker, it may lie down as soon as it enters dense cover.

Standing corn is a welcome sight to any wounded deer. Deer visit these fields with consistency, bedding and feeding in them whenever they are available. When wounded, and particularly when they know a tracker is on their tail, they will seek the security of standing corn. A cornfield is like a big thicket, and a deer knows it can hide there.

Wounded deer often seek the security of standing corn. If the deer you are tracking suddenly goes into a standing cornfield, proceed slowly and quietly, listening for sounds of stalks breaking, and watching closely for blood smears on stalks.

If you track a deer into standing corn, look for blood smears on the stalks. If the ground is bare, you will probably find little or no blood. Always listen for sounds of crushing stalks after you have entered a standing cornfield. If you come across the bed of a wounded deer, look for bent over or broken stalks to determine the direction it traveled after leaving the bed.

Anytime you find a bed with blood in it, regardless of its location, look closely for another nearby. It could be the deer got up and moved only a few yards before lying down again. I sometimes find four or five beds when tracking a gut-shot deer, though two or three is more common. On one occasion, I found eleven beds before making the recovery.

You should always examine a bed closely before looking for another bed nearby, or for the blood trail leading away. You will sometimes find hair, smeared blood, or even a pool of blood. By examining the location of the blood in the bed, you may determine the kind of wound you are dealing with. Keep in mind that deer beds are slightly oval, with the hips forming the large end of the bed.

When a deer lies down, its bed is oval shaped. If you find a bed with blood in it, examine closely to see if the blood is near the narrow or wide end of the bed. The hips of the deer will make the wide portion of the bed.

The more time a deer spends in a bed, the better the chance the blood will coagulate. I can't tell you how many times I have followed a heavy blood trail to a bed, but couldn't find another drop after that. For this reason, look for tracks leading away from the bed, as well as blood smears on debris surrounding the bed. You can bet there is blood on the deer's hide that may wipe off on something it bumps against when it leaves the bed. It's important that you know the direction the deer traveled when it left the bed. The direction it came from has nothing to do with the direction it went upon leaving the bed, providing you did not spook the deer.

If you jump the deer and cannot get another shot, watch it carefully as it departs. Pay special attention to the direction it goes, and its agility. This may tell you if the deer will travel only a short distance and bed down again.

Do Deer Circle?

I have read many tracking articles over the years. Some authors claim that deer do circle back, close to where they were shot; others say "absolutely not." As for my personal experiences, I'm convinced that some do-providing opportunity allows and certain conditions exist.

Many years ago, I shot a doe just before dusk. She left the scene as if hit hard. Thirty minutes after dark, a couple of friends and I started tracking. Two hundred yards later, we found my arrow. It had totally penetrated the deer, but the blood was bright. A lung shot was ruled out because the deer had already moved 100 yards farther than it should have.

We lost the trail near midnight, so I returned with a friend the next morning. I spent the entire day tracking the deer, ending up about three-fourths of a mile away. I returned again the next day and tracked the deer for six more hours, finally losing the blood trail about seventy-five yards from where the doe stood when I shot her two days ago. I never recovered the deer, and suspected my arrow had passed through heavy muscle where the neck joins the shoulder. However, this was my first experience of a deer making a large circle, and it provided me with a bit of education.

It's no big news that deer seldom run a straight line after being wounded. Many lung and heart-shot deer will, simply because they flee the scene quickly, and their time runs out. However, most deer will always circle slightly after running a distance of 200 yards or more.

Although some deer do circle back after being shot, many do not. The possibility of a deer circling depends upon how far you track the deer, as well as the animal's home range.

The number of deer that circle back to the same proximity where they were shot is anyone's guess. No deer does this quickly, however. If the wounded deer travels several hundred yards or more, it may end up close to where it was shot, such as the doe mentioned previously. Was this doe an exception? I doubt it. In fact, since that time, I have followed many blood trails that circled back. However, only those deer I followed for long distances made a circle, or showed signs of circling before the trail expired. I believe that most blood trails may be lost before the hunter has figured out that a deer is going to circle back. In other cases, the hunter may recover the deer before the animal begins to make a distinct circle. Nonetheless, many deer that receive minor wounds, or those that are pushed, do circle back.

During the rut, I have seen many bucks travel a near straight line for a long distance, particularly when pushed by trackers. I assume these bucks might have been searching for does far from their home range when wounded, and may have a desire to head back to their home range. It could be, too, that they feel secure in their home range, knowing this is where they spend much of their time. I've also noticed that some bucks during the early archery season tended to circle back after traveling a short distance. I suspect this is because they were already close to their home range where they bedded consistently only days or weeks earlier.

If a deer is severely wounded, I doubt that circling back is a concern. If it wants to bed down, it will do so when the first opportunity allows.

Uphill and Downhill Facts

I have seen many deer go uphill, even when mortally wounded. I once helped a friend track a stomach-shot deer in the big hills of Kentucky at Land Between the Lakes. A few hours after he shot the deer, we picked up the trail and followed it about 200 yards along the base of a big ridge. There was just enough blood getting to the ground to stay on the trail. However, after the blood trail expired, we spent more than an hour searching ahead, hoping for one more droplet that would put us back on track. Eventually, I returned to the last drop and looked up the side of the steep ridge. It looked scuffed, as if a deer had walked up, so I thought it best to take a closer look. A few minutes later I arrived on top of the hill, only to see the buck in a bed. He was bedded near the top of the hill and had watched me approach. I slowly backed off and went down the hill to get my friend. A short time later, my friend walked to the top of the hill, found the deer still alive, and finished it off.

When a deer goes up and down hills or embankments, most of the blood is found at the top or the bottom and not along the side of the hill. Although blood trails are usually weak when a deer travels uphill or downhill, I have found that most deer leave better blood trails walking downhill than they do when they go uphill. It would seem that their heart rate would increase more when going uphill, thus causing more external blood loss, but this is not usually the case. The hunter must simply remember that a deer may go up or down a hill, even if mortally wounded.

Wounded deer sometimes go uphill or downhill when wounded. Blood is more likely to be found on the top or bottom of the hill than on its sides.

Wounded Deer Do Swim

Common sense often depicts things that are not true. For instance, many hunters refuse to believe a severely injured deer would go up a steep hill. Some hunters cannot fathom a deer jumping in a body of water and swimming to the other side when severely wounded. Nevertheless, they do. Probably not very often, but it's best that you don't rule it out. I have tracked at least two deer that swam bodies of water. On one occasion, my nephew shot a buck that went into a lake and came out the other side. The lake was small and the buck knew that we were on his trail. I believe he did this in an attempt to lose us. I don't think a deer is capable of reasoning, but I do believe their instincts tell them that we follow them by scent, just as they follow other deer and as they are followed by predators. The wounded buck I just mentioned had no reason to swim across the lake, except to lose us. He could have easily walked around it and reached the other side just as quickly. By the way, we did pick up blood on the other side of the lake a short distance from where the deer came out of the water. Unfortunately, we lost the trail 200 yards later and never recovered the buck.

A southern Indiana bowhunter suspected the deer he shot swam across a large strip-mined lake. After finding blood and tracks at water's edge, he marked the spot and put a boat in the lake up ahead. He maneuvered the boat along the lake until he reached the marker. Once there, he guided the boat across the lake and began looking for blood and tracks along the edge of the water. However, a surprise greeted him. He found the buck lying in the water by the lake's edge. The 100-yard swim apparently did the buck in. The arrow had passed through its liver.

Yes, a wounded deer will go across water if wants to. Perhaps it happens when a deer wants to get back into its home range. Perhaps it only happens when it knows that a hunter is on its trail.

Big Bucks Die Hard

Throughout this book, I mention various types of wounds and how far a deer might travel. I based these calculations upon tracking experiences with adult deer, and then averaged them to get the results. However, I have found that the size of the deer will have much to do with how far it goes before bedding, or dying when a severe wound occurs. Big bucks seem to go farther than most adult whit tails, while six-month-old deer seem to travel less distance, even when identical wounds exist.

"Big bucks die hard," Tim Hillsmeyer, an experienced deer hunter from southern Indiana, once told me. I didn't dispute Tim's word, but I wondered how a deer that had a liver wound and/or stomach wound could survive for so many hours.

The buck I'm referring to was shot one morning and recovered the next. I recover most liver-shot deer within a couple of hours. However, this buck, a four-and-one-half-year-old deer, field dressed at 189 pounds and carried an eleven-point rack. I jumped the buck six hours after my Muzzy broadhead had passed through his liver. After marking the bed, I returned with my wife and Tim the following morning. We found the buck piled up about 150 yards from where I had jumped him. You can read the details of this tracking episode in Chapter 12.

In 1990, I shot a huge Alberta whitetail buck while bowhunting with Jim Hole, Jr. of Classic Outfitters. The double lung-shot deer ran 150 yards. While that is not a long distance, it is farther than most adult whitetails travel after an arrow zips through both lungs. I estimated the northern buck would probably field dress about 240 pounds. Jim later told me that it is common for big Alberta bucks to travel that far when mortally wounded.

Nevertheless, I have seen young deer die sooner than adult deer, providing of course the broadhead or projectile hits the body cavity. As a rule, most six-month-old deer will succumb sooner, and travel less distance than an adult deer when lung shot, liver shot, or stomach shot.

The moral to this story? Don't become discouraged if you shoot a big buck and thought you hit it well, only to find yourself tracking farther than you anticipated. Every hunter should be aware that big deer probably have more stamina than little deer.

Tracking in the Dark

I can't begin to recall every nighttime tracking job I've been on. My most recent experience occurred just last year, when my wife shot a buck right before dusk. We tracked the deer for about three hours before giving up the trail until the following morning.

Southern Indiana deer hunter Tim Hillsmeyer has taken numerous trophy whitetails. He claims that many big bucks "die hard." In other words, they may travel those few extra yards, even when hit hard.

Tracking in the dark is usually less productive than daytime trailing if the deer has sustained a wound other than a double lung hit. Naturally, vision is a problem. You can't see far, blood is often more difficult to find, markers don't show up well, you will probably have no idea if the wounded deer is getting out of a bed a short distance ahead, and it's difficult to determine the direction the deer is traveling unless you consistently use a compass. Nonetheless, there is a positive side of night trailing. If you shoot a deer in the evening, the blood may still be wet. If you let the deer go until morning, blood droplets will be dry. As you probably know, wet blood shows up much easier than dried blood. It could be, too, that the wound calls for immediate and slow tracking. If you let the deer go until dawn, coagulation will probably occur overnight. However, some wounds require you to wait until morning, no questions asked. One example is a deer that has an abdominal wound.

When you must track a deer at night, you should use lights that will make it easier for you to see blood. Small handheld flashlights are fine for getting to and from your stand in the dark, but they don't help much when you're looking for blood. Gas-powered lanterns provide excellent illumination and cover a wider area.

Rechargeable lights also do a good job of lighting up a large area. I keep The Wizard Topper, manufactured by Nite Lite, in my vehicle throughout the hunting season. The six-volt rechargeable battery provides several hours of light when fully charged. And believe me, you never know just how many hours you might be in the woods when a night tracking job begins. In looking back, I tracked at least one deer in the dark for more than six hours.

Even if you don't suspect a good hit, and you don't intend to track the deer after dark, the right light makes it possible for you to look for blood, hair, or even a spent arrow. It is sometimes necessary to find such evidence to determine the type of wound you are dealing with. If you do find evidence that suggests a good hit, such as bright blood, then you would probably want to track the deer immediately. Why risk something going wrong overnight? You should always consider weather, coyotes, and coagulation. However, I have found that you can do a better job of examining an arrow for blood and hair inside the house under a bright light.

You will be surprised how different everything looks in the dark. Getting lost is probably ten times easier in the dark than in the daylight. Therefore, I would suggest you carry a compass and take a reading before you begin tracking. Walking around carelessly and wondering where you are is one sure way to trample over a blood trail, or spook a deer away that may have been bedded nearby.

When I'm in unfamiliar territory, I often carry a spool of line from a string-tracking device. It provides several hundred yards of line. I tie it onto a handy obstacle at the beginning of a blood trail, and let it out as I track the deer. I always retrieve the line after I finish tracking a deer.

It helps to have one or two others along when tracking a deer at dark. Each person should stay close, perhaps within forty or fifty yards of each other at all times. If you have tracked a deer after dark, you already know how easily the light your buddy carries can vanish. Each person should use his ears as well as his eyes. You may hear the deer ahead of you, getting out of a bed, walking or running. If you find your deer after dark, but don't intend to get it out until the next morning, use tissue paper or trail marking ribbon to mark the spot where the deer lies, or a trail leading to the deer. This will make it easier for you when you return the next morning. If predators could find your deer, consider laying a piece of clothing over the animal. The human scent keeps predators at bay. Always assume that tracking after dark will take three times longer than you anticipate. I've had to eat a few burnt suppers over the years, thanks to nighttime tracking. Many times, I have called home and explained that I would be an hour late. However, short tracking jobs often turn into more than a few frustrating hours of tracking.

When tracking a deer after dark, use a light that will illuminate an area fully. Many trackers prefergas powered lanterns or rechargeable lights.

Weather Effects

Mother Nature can turn a normal tracking job into a nightmare in a hurry. The hunter must always be concerned with rain, snow, frost, and temperature. It can work in your favor, or it can work against you.

Obviously, rain or snow can wipe a blood trail clean. However, a frost or hard freeze can also affect a blood trail. Blood darkens after freezing, or after being smothered with a gentle frost. The dark blood can be misleading, and cause you to believe that you have a liver or gut-shot wound to deal with, instead of a wound that produces bright blood. For this reason, always consider that a blood trail may look different in the morning than it did the previous evening.

Blood in woods and dense thickets may not be affected by a light frost like blood in open areas. However, any blood trail will be affected by a hard freeze.

If rain or snow is forecast, and the deer you shot has a wound that requires you to wait for a few hours to begin tracking, a question arises. Should you take your chances and track the animal now to beat the snow and rain, or do you wait and hope for the best?

Snow or rain can turn your tracking endeavor into a nightmare. Despite this, the author steadfastly refuses to track gut-shot deer immediately, even when rain or snow is in the forecast.

Several years ago, I would track a deer immediately if rain or snow was in the forecast. However, I no longer abide by that rule unless immediate tracking is called for. If I am certain the deer was hit in the stomach or intestines, I will avoid tracking the animal for several hours, regardless of the forecast. Even if there is a 100 percent chance of rain, I refuse to track a gut-shot deer right away. This takes perseverance, but I'm convinced it is the right choice.

About fifteen years ago, I released my arrow at an eight-pointer about twenty minutes before dark. With the deer standing only fifteen yards away, I positively determined that my arrow passed through the deer's abdomen. Just before dark, I climbed down and retrieved the arrow. It was laced with stomach contents and specks of dark blood.

After hearing that the forecast called for rain, I returned one hour later with a couple of other hunters and started tracking the deer. We tediously followed the skimpy blood trail for 100 yards, only to jump the buck in the dark. Light rain had started falling, so we continued tracking the deer. We jumped the buck again thirty minutes later. We found no blood beyond the buck's second bed, and were eventually forced to call off the tracking endeavor.

When I returned the following morning, I could find no blood or tracks leading away from the second bed. After an all-day search proved fruitless, I gave up, even though I knew the deer would not survive the wound.

I found the buck a few days later, only fifty yards from the tree stand where I took the shot. The deer had obviously turned back toward my stand after we jumped him from his second bed, traveled a short distance, laid down, and died. Had I not have pursued the buck the night before, I'm certain it could have been found in or near the first bed.

Today, I won't immediately track any deer that has received an abdomen wound. Since many of these deer bed down within a short distance of where they are shot, and since it could take a few hours for them to succumb, it makes no sense to push the animal farther away just because your blood trail could dissipate within a few hours. If rain does wash away the blood trail, I will come back with others and search the area thoroughly.

A light rain does not always wash out a blood trail. Of course, the more blood that gets to the ground, the better the chance that some will still be there a few hours after the rain stops. A downpour will be much more damaging to the blood trail, but even then, you may find blood in a bed. Pools of blood left in beds often survive a heavy rain, even if the blood trail is abolished.

I have tracked some deer (those with muscular wounds) during rain, and watched the blood trail slowly diminish right before my eyes. Each drop becomes watered down until it vanishes. When rain falls while Iím tracking a deer, I mark my trail every few yards, assuming I may soon have to begin a recovery effort based on the directional travel of the deer. Snow can have a severe effect, since it covers blood. Additionally, a deer that died and cooled out before the snow started falling can be covered and difficult to see.

A gun hunter may choose to track a deer right away if bad weather is forecast, providing it is daylight. It's unlawful to take a gun in the field after dark to track a deer, but during daylight hours, you can consider tracking the animal before bad weather arrives, and hope for a second shot.

Warm temperatures are another concern, since a deer could spoil if you don't recover it soon enough. However, this will still not prompt me to track a deer with an abdominal wound. I feel confident that it will take a few hours for the deer to succumb, and will wait the necessary hours to begin tracking. If I shoot a deer at dusk and the temperature will not drop below fifty degrees (ten Celsius), I may wait a few hours and return later that night to begin tracking. Although a deer may bloat, it does not always mean that the meat has gone bad.

Terrain Effects

Terrain can affect the amount of blood you find, or the appearance of the blood. For instance, when you track a deer across soil, and there are no leaves or debris on the ground, the blood usually appears darker. It is also more difficult to see when it lands on soil. Thus, if a blood trail that was easy to follow suddenly ends up in such an area, you can assume the blood is probably still there but harder to find. You will then need to trail slowly to make certain you don't lose the trail before the deer reaches an area where the blood begins to show up. Except for snow and harvested cornfield stalks, nothing shows blood better than leaves. I do love tracking a deer across cornfields, since the blood can be readily spotted on the dry, yellow stalks. Blood also shows on honeysuckle. The dark-green leaves make a good background for the red blood.

Any tracker appreciates leaves when tracking a deer. However, if the deer suddenly moves across bare soil, continue slowly and get close to the ground. Be aware that blood may appear darker on soil than on leaves.

Pine thickets are usually poor places to find blood, since the blood seems to pass through pine needles and into the soil. Pastures and other fields also create problems. It is usually disappointing to follow a blood trail to an open field, whether it is a pasture or a high weed field, simply because the trailing may become difficult. It is also possible that you can see across the field for a long distance, and know that the deer is not there. Then you realize that the real work is about to begin. You must then become persistent, and do your best to pick up the trail and follow it across the field. Many wounded deer, upon entering a field, will not move across an entire field. Instead, they may go into the field only a short distance and turn sharply toward cover along the edge.

I would assume that many wounded deer do not like crossing fields. Most deer shot through the body cavity want to stay in cover. However, even if a mortally wounded deer is pushed, it will not hesitate to go into a field when that is what it needs to do to get away from the tracker.

Tracking a deer in an open field can become very discouraging. If you lose the blood trail, check the adjoining cover for blood droplets and smears.

Blood is much more difficult to detect on deer trails of dirt or mud. A tracker must slow his pace considerably in order not to overlook blood signs.

Chapter 7

Cardiorespiratory Wounds

Most hunters consider a deer's lungs and heart the primary target, and rightfully so. In most cases, the animal will not travel far with a wound to these organs. However, there are exceptions. For instance, some heart-shot deer do not drop dead in their tracks, or fall dead after running fifty to 100 yards. It's also true that a deer shot in only one lung will travel a long distance and can be very difficult to recover.

Before discussing lung and heart hits, let me first clarify that mistakes can be made when judging these wounds. Over the years, I've heard stories from hunters who said they hit a deer squarely in both lungs, only to track the animal for a long distance and never recover it. I don't get into a heated debate with a hunter who tells me this. Nevertheless, I will ask the hunter if he could have made an error when he assumed the hit. You know how it goes: You shoot at a deer and watch your arrow pass through its front section, and assume you hit both lungs. A short time later, you find yourself tracking the deer for a considerable distance, wondering what is going on and why the deer has not yet dropped. However, no deer is a supernatural creature, capable of surviving without breathing.

The truth is, no deer will survive with a hole in both lungs. If the deer does not go down, you can safely assume you did not hit both lungs. One lung, maybe. It's also possible that a projectile or broadhead can hit high behind the shoulder and miss the lungs entirely. Many hunters refer to this as a "black hole." The black hole can also become a hunter's nightmare. This wound misleads you from the beginning, and often guides you into a long tracking adventure, with no deer at the end of the trail. Here's a look at what you can expect when you hit both lungs.

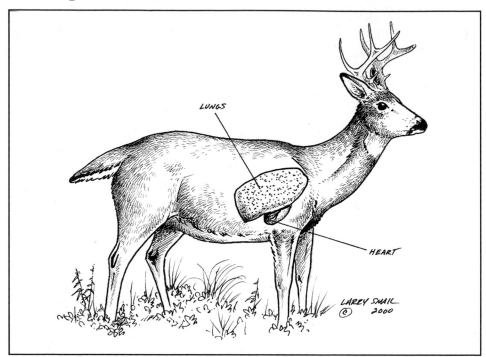

LUNGS

HEART

LARRY SMAIL
© 2000

The preferred shot is the lungs and heart. Although a wound to both lungs will result in a quick, clean kill, some heart-shot deer may travel farther than anticipated.

Double-Lung Shot

The lungs of a deer are shaped like footballs. Each lung is roughly the size of a nine-inch pie plate, and takes up a large portion of the chest cavity. When air comes into the lungs through the bronchus, each lung forms air sacs, which are surrounded by capillaries. When a vertebrate animal inhales, the lungs expand. When the animal exhales, the lungs contract.

Your best opportunity to hit both lungs is when the animal is standing broadside. A slightly quartering-away deer also offers a direct path for the broadhead or projectile. Even if you hit the quartering-away deer in the middle of the abdomen, your arrow or bullet will get into the boiler room, taking out other organs along the way. If the deer quarters away sharply, or quarters to you, it becomes almost impossible to hit both lungs.

When a deer is hit in the lungs, and the heart and aorta artery is spared, it usually lunges forward and goes into a hard run, much like that of a racehorse coming down the home stretch. Its belly is also low to the ground as it takes long strides. A deer may go over the top of bushes, and may leap over brushpiles that are in the way. When the deer begins running, the tail is often up about halfway. After the animal runs thirty to forty yards, the tail usually drops. These are the typical reactions.

If the shoulder is missed, a lung-shot deer will usually run full-speed ahead. There are exceptions to this rule, however.

Some lung-shot deer, particularly when wounded by an arrow, may only lunge forward and stand still, or run just a few yards and stop. Some even snort when hit. Although the latter mentioned reactions are uncommon, they can and have occurred.

The distance a double-lung shot deer will travel varies, depending upon body size, and the size of the hole in the lungs. As mentioned in the previous chapter, I have seen exceptionally big bucks travel up to 150 yards. The average adult deer will go about 100 yards, however. A young deer may also travel a shorter distance than an adult. I saw one young deer run only thirty yards after an arrow zipped through both lungs. Of course, breaking a shoulder could drop the animal, or cause it to go down, get back up and run. Death usually comes within thirty seconds.

Most deer hit in both lungs slow and begin staggering just before they go down. I have heard some cough. When a deer coughs at the moment of death, it is not as loud as that of many black bears I have heard. When both lungs are hit, a deer will hemorrhage and suffocate rapidly.

I have heard some hunters say that a low-lung hit is better than a high-lung shot. I must agree. I have noticed that most deer hit in the lower portion of the chest cavity seem to travel slightly less distance than those hit in the upper half of the lungs, even when the arrow or bullet did not hit the heart. Regardless of whether you hit high or low in the lungs, the deer will go down quickly.

The height of your entry and departure holes will determine how quickly blood gets to the ground. When a deer is hit in both lungs, you might find blood within twenty yards of where you shot the deer. A low shot in the lungs could allow you to find blood within five to ten yards. However, you could also find hair where the deer stood when you shot. The hair of a chest hit will be dark brown or gray, very coarse, medium to long in length with black tips. The higher up the chest you hit the deer, the longer the hair.

If a lung-shot deer runs out of sight, I don't wait long to begin tracking. In fact, when sure of the hit, I will usually begin looking for sign within twenty minutes. If there is any doubt, and the possibility exists that my arrow or bullet hit farther back, I will wait longer before moving to the location where the deer was hit. I see it like this: If I hit the lungs, the animal is down and not going anywhere. If I missed the vital lungs and hit the liver or stomach, I should delay tracking for a reasonable time.

The blood of a lung-shot deer is bright red, and may look pink. You may find foamy blood, but usually not until the deer has run fifty or more yards. Many times, a hunter may not see foamy blood because he spots the downed deer and advances ahead without looking for more blood. A tracker commonly finds foamy blood along the last few yards of the trail. A bowhunter that finds his arrow, though, may see foamy blood on the shaft.

Do not confuse foamy blood with other air bubbles that sometimes appear in blood droplets. Many times, when tracking deer with muscle wounds, I have found large splotches of blood that contained a few tiny air bubbles. In some cases, I was even fooled into believing a lung shot occurred. However, foamy blood consists of a large mass of air bubbles.

The blood trail of a lung-shot deer usually becomes more obvious as you follow it. The blood often blows out to the sides of the deer's route, sometimes a couple of feet from the animal's tracks. You may find blood splattered high on bush-es, as well as on the ground. The lower in the chest you hit the deer, the better the blood trail. However, the trail of any double-lung shot deer is easy to follow, unless you shoot the deer straight down under a tree and the arrow or projectile does not come out the bottom.

The One-Lung Hit

A deer shot in only one lung seldom results in a happy experience. The deer may cause you to think that a recovery is about to occur, but in most situations it does not. In fact, I have far more faith in recovering a gut-shot deer than one hit in one lung. And believe me, I've had my experiences with one-lung shot deer.

It is not unusual to find blood a couple of feet to the sides of a deer's tracks, when it's hit through both lungs. You might also find foamy blood, but usually it will be farther down the trail, close to where the animal drops. (Photo by Vikki L. Trout)

Two years before writing this book, a beautiful ten-point buck walked down a steep embankment and stopped only five yards from my tree stand. He was just about eye level, and I was sitting down and not prepared. A moment later, the deer turned broadside, took a couple of steps, then stopped and looked back from where he came. From a sitting position, I drew my bowstring and attempted to settle my sight pin just behind his shoulder. A small tree covered the pathway to his lungs, so I just eased the pin to the right a couple of inches, and released the arrow on the shoulder. I have made many shoulder shots on deer when bowhunting, and usually my arrow penetrated into the lungs. This time, things went differently. The arrow hit precisely where I aimed, but penetrated only about five inches. The buck lunged forward and ran hard, over the hill and out of sight. Meanwhile, I sat in my stand hoping I had somehow hit both lungs.

After tracking the deer for about 150 yards, I soon got the picture. I had hit only one lung, and my tracking skills were about to be tested to the max. Rather than give you the discouraging details that followed, let me just say that I spent about fourteen hours tracking this deer. By the end of the second day, I had jumped the buck once, found two beds, and lost the blood trail. This is what can happen when a one-lung hit occurs.

On the other hand, deer hit in only one lung are sometimes recovered. I've been fortunate to see a few recoveries, and I am always anxious to congratulate the successful hunter when the tracking is over. Even the best trackers will have a difficult time locating a deer hit in one lung.

John Maltby, Supervisory Veterinary Medical Officer/Circuit Supervisor with the U.S. Dept. of Agriculture, said it may be possible for a deer to survive when only one lung is wounded.

Tracking a deer hit in only one lung is often tedious work. This deer is difficult to recover and may travel a considerable distance before bedding down. If one lung collapses, the other will usually continue to function.

"Humans have what is called a mediastina that separates their lungs, which means that if one lung collapses, it's not going to affect the other lung," explained Maltby. "Not every animal has this complete membrane between the lungs. In some animals, such as dogs, a wound to only one lung will cause both lungs to collapse."

While doing anatomy research for this book, I was not able to determine if deer have a mediastina. Deer do have a diaphragm, which separates the abdominal and thoracic cavities. However, if one considers the difficulty of recovering a deer shot in only one lung, it would appear the membrane does exist. Maltby said that if this is the case, it would seem reasonable that with enough adrenaline, the lung that was not wounded will continue to do the job.

The best possibility of hitting only one lung is when you shoot at a deer quartering to or away from you. The latter shot is better, since you could hit other vital organs.

The reactions of a deer hit in only one lung are similar to that of the double-lung shot deer. The color of the blood is bright red. You may find blood close to the location you shot the deer. Again, just how close you find it depends upon the height of the hole, or number of holes in the deer. You seldom find foamy blood when tracking a deer hit in only one lung, although you might find blood with numerous air bubbles.

The blood trail of a deer hit in only one lung is not like that of a deer shot in both lungs. The trail may intensify for a short distance, after the deer runs fifty to 100 yards, but will soon taper off. This deer will usually stop and start walking after it runs 100 yards, and may bed down shortly thereafter.

I prefer to push the one-lung shot deer slowly and quietly. This slows coagulation, and increases blood loss, both internally and externally. If I jump the deer from a bed, I may wait up to thirty minutes and start tracking again. A deer hit in one lung will probably not succumb, but patiently pushing the deer will increase your chances of a recovery.

Heart Shots

The heart of an adult deer is slightly oval, five to six inches long and about four inches wide, and located low in the chest cavity. An arrow or bullet that enters a deer near the brisket, just behind the front leg, is certain to pierce the heart. I'll take a heart shot any day, but I still prefer the lungs. Allow me to explain.

I've heard hunters brag about shooting a deer in the heart. I agree; the heart is a good place to hit a deer, and worth bragging about. It beats the heck out of hitting the animal too far back. However, some hunters claim they shoot for the heart. I can't understand this, considering the lungs are much larger and offer room for error. If you shoot for the center of the chest, forward in the deer, you can spare a few inches in any direction. If you shoot for the heart, you could miss entirely or even hit the front leg if your arrow or bullet strays slightly.

Another factor comes to mind. A heart-shot deer does not always go down as quickly as a lung-shot deer. There have been many claims of heart-shot deer running 200 yards. In other cases, death was prolonged and the animal actu-ally bedded down. I remember one such incident several years ago, when my dad and I hunted whitetails in Pennsylvania during the early archery season.

One evening, my dad shot a small buck after it came in to browse on apples littered about an old orchard. He hit the deer low, behind the front leg, and suspected a heart shot. He waited a few minutes before tracking the deer, assuming he would soon fill his tag. However, near dusk he came up on the bedded buck. Since he had left his bow behind, he sat down, stayed hidden a short distance away, and watched the deer. At dark, the deer was still alive. Dad left to get the rest of us, assuming the deer would be dead when we returned.

Forty-five minutes later, we arrived on the scene. The buck was lying on his side and now dead. Of coarse, Dad had begun to think that the arrow had somehow missed the heart. When we field-dressed the deer, we examined the heart and found a neat slice on one side. The broadhead did not put a hole in the heart, but the wound to the heart, which proved to be severe, allowed the animal to live for more than an hour.

A heart-shot deer will often kick out its back legs, and run hard but very erratically, sometimes lunging in different directions.

I seriously doubt that anyone can explain how a pierced heart can go on beating for more than a few seconds. However, for some strange reason, it can. Perhaps if the damage to the heart is extremely traumatic, it will stop beating and cause circulation to cease sooner than a lesser traumatic wound. Once circulation stops, oxygen is no longer carried to the brain, and the deer will die. Nonetheless, I will track the heart-shot deer immediately, but be on the lookout for a moving deer just in case the heart is only nicked.

If a wound to the heart is the result of a low hit, and does not stem from an angled shot higher up on the deer, blood is usually found within ten to twenty yards of where the animal was standing when the hunter took the shot. The blood is bright to crimson red. It is also common for the blood to splatter a few feet away from the deer's trail. The blood trail is very steady, and profuse external bleeding is com-mon when there is a low hole in the deer. Nevertheless, there are exceptions, such as if a deer's leg slides across the entry or departure hole each time it takes a step. This often causes a weaker blood trail, as the leg prevents blood from getting to the ground.

A bowhunter may find specks of tallow on his arrow after a heart shot, providing it passes through the heart first and the brisket of the deer last. The brisket contains a pocket of tallow, as does a portion of the deer's body near the back, and on the underside of the neck (these wounds and tallow are discussed in Chapter 9, on muscular and skeletal wounds).

Tallow is off-white in color, very thick, and somewhat sticky. The best way to see it is on a dark-colored shaft under a good light. You can also feel the tallow. If you run a finger over the shaft, the tallow will feel greasy, and the shaft slightly lumpy. A hunter may become discouraged upon finding tallow on an arrow shaft, and rightfully so, as it usually represents a superficial brisket wound.

One exception occurred many years ago when my friend, Mark Williams, shot a doe. His arrow was loaded with flecks of tallow from the nock to the broad-head, and you could find only a trace of blood on the shaft. It looked as though he had made a perfect brisket shot. However, the blood trail got better after we had followed it for seventy-five yards. After tracking the deer 125 yards, we found the doe quite dead. The entrance hole of the arrow was about two inches above the bottom of the deer, just behind the front leg. The exit hole was on the underneath side of the deer, only about four inches from the entry hole.

A heart-shot deer may run hard, but the deer with only a brisket wound usually lopes off, or lunges forward and stands. The blood trail of a brisket wound and a brisket/heart wound differs totally. A wound to only the brisket usually results in a few drops of blood and a short tracking endeavor. In fact, the blood trail often ceases after 100 yards. There are exceptions, however, such as a long scrape wound across the bottom of the brisket. This wound causes substantial bleeding, and usually results in an easy-to-follow trail for more than 100 yards. Coagulation soon becomes a factor, though, and the bleeding stops by the time the deer travels 150 to 200 yards. A brisket/heart wound will leave an obvious blood trail, and eventually lead to a deer.

One noticeable mark of the heart-shot deer is its initial reaction to the shot, and its run that follows. Many heart-shot deer will kick their hind hooves outwards when hit, as if they just received an electric shock. The deer will then run hard, but erratically. I have seen some heart-shot deer jerk back and forth from side to side as they ran away.

You may find hair where you shot the deer, particularly if your bullet or broadhead comes out on the brisket of the deer. The hair of a heart-shot deer is similar to that of a lung-shot deer - dark brown or gray, and coarse with black tips, except not as long. Hair from the brisket is similar to heart hair, but is slightly longer, very thick, and stiff. It may even curl.

Windpipe (Trachea)

A wound to the windpipe will also include a wound to neck muscles, which can cause profuse bleeding. However, it is also possible that the carotid artery, jugular vein, and/or neck vertebrate would be hit. The angle of the shot will determine whether you hit only the windpipe and neck muscles.

What are your chances of recovering a deer that receives only a wound to the windpipe and neck muscles? It could very well depend upon the extent of damage to the windpipe.

According to Maltby, it may be possible for a deer to survive a minor wound to the windpipe. He claimed that if the windpipe were crushed, death would come quickly because the animal could not breathe. A minor wound could be classified as a nick, or slight cut. Air may still flow through the windpipe, despite bleeding.

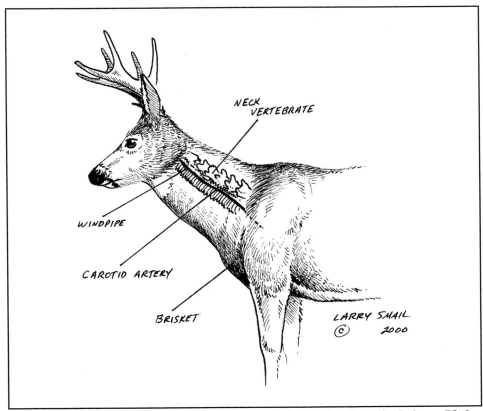

It is difficult for a broadhead or bullet to hit only the windpipe. If the windpipe is severed, the carotid artery or the neck vertebrate may also be hit. However, the neck should not be your choice of shots.

A wound to the windpipe will result in bright-red blood due to severed muscles in the neck. You may find a few air bubbles in the blood, but not like the foamy blood that occurs when you hit both lungs.

I have participated in the tracking of several deer that received neck wounds. In cases where we didn't recover the deer in a short distance, such as when a major artery is not severed, I could assume only a wound to neck muscles. However, I have also found air bubbles in blood droplets when tracking deer with neck wounds. This may or may not have been the result of a minor cut to the windpipe.

Conclusion

This chapter discussed clues that can help you to determine whether you made a positive hit, and tracking suggestions for a wound to the thoracic cavity or windpipe. The bright and crimson blood that comes from these wounds is similar to that of many muscular wounds, however. Therefore, examine hair if you find it, take note to the deer's reaction when shot, and the appearance of the blood trail before coming to a conclusion about the wound

Chapter 8

Abdominal Wounds

The abdominal cavity is directly behind the deer's thoracic cavity, and is separated by the diaphragm. Several organs are found in the abdominal cavity, such as the liver, stomach, spleen, intestines, and kidneys. A wound to any of these organs is sure to result in death, although some abdominal wounds do not kill as quickly as others do.

All too often, hunters use the term "gut shot" and "paunch shot" after hitting a deer in the abdominal cavity. However, not all wounds to the abdomen result in a gut-shot or paunch-shot deer. For the sake of being on the same wave length, I will refer to the stomach and intestines as the guts, or paunch. Equally important is that other organs in the abdominal cavity, such as the liver and kidneys, should not be considered as part of the guts, or paunch.

It's vital that you are aware of the location of the organs in the abdominal cavity, and how a wound to one organ might differ from another. For instance, if you hit a deer in the liver, you will find that the tracking will go much smoother than if you were tracking a deer shot in the intestines, and that death will come much sooner. On the other hand, a kidney-shot deer differs from a liver-shot deer in that a kidney wound causes death within seconds. In addition, the color of blood can vary, depending upon the abdominal organ that is punctured.

A shot to the abdominal cavity might also result in a wound to more than one organ. Thus, you could find variations in blood color when you track the deer, and experience a tracking situation different than you anticipated. You may not discover which organs were hit until you field dress the deer, so it may help your future tracking endeavors to examine the animal closely after making a recovery.

Liver Wounds

I prefer hitting the liver of a deer much more than the stomach or intestines. The blood trail is usually better, and the animal usually succumbs in less time. However, I have seen some liver-shot deer travel farther than I ever believed they would, particularly some exceptionally big bucks. In Chapter 11, I provide the details of a monster buck that survived for many hours. I mention this now, just to let you know that exceptions do exist.

A liver-shot deer will surely die, usually within a few hours. Internal bleed-ing begins the moment the liver is punctured. Most liver-shot deer I have tracked were dead within one to two hours.

The liver is the largest organ, about ten by six inches in an adult deer. It serves many functions in the digestive system, and it stores vitamins and minerals. It lies neatly in a vertical position just behind the diaphragm, close to the middle of the deer. Because of its vertical position and overlapping lobe, a broadhead or projectile will seldom find its way between the narrow boundaries of the liver. A quartering shot, though, can easily result in a liver wound.

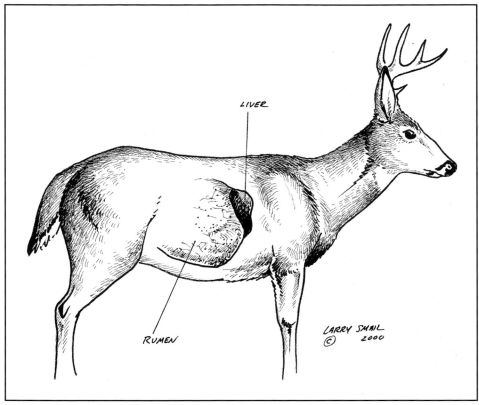

The liver is just behind the diaphragm, which separates the abdominal and thoracic cavities. Because of the liver's vertical position, an arrow or broadhead seldom hits it unless the deer quarters into or away from the hunter.

If a hunter shoots at a broadside deer and the shot is not too low, he may hit the liver if his arrow or projectile hits just inches behind the lungs. Oftentimes, a bowhunter may believe he hit the lungs, only to discover a liver wound once he tracks or recovers the animal.

If you hit a deer in the middle of its body, and do not punch out on the bottom of the animal, you may find hair similar to that of a lung wound. The hair is very coarse, medium length, and dark brown or gray with black tips. The best possibility of finding the hair of a liver-shot deer is at the location where the deer stood when shot, on the broadhead or nock of an arrow, or in a bed.

When the liver is hit, a deer usually lunges ahead quickly and runs away hard, but not as fast as a lung-shot deer. However, it typically runs harder than a stomach- or intestine-shot deer. A liver-shot deer will not run a short distance, stop, and stand for a while, as many gut-shot deer do.

The blood of a liver-shot deer is dark red, appearing almost maroon. However, it is not as dark as that of a gut-shot deer. Judging the color of blood is easiest when you see a bloody arrow, or blood on the ground before it dries.

A liver-shot deer should be recovered within 250 yards, provided you do not push it. Most deer will bed down after moving 150 yards or less.

It is common for a liver-shot deer to bleed externally after it runs about thirty or forty yards. You'll rarely find blood on the spot where you shot the deer, however. The volume of blood that follows the first few droplets will depend upon a couple of factors. For one, if the stomach is also punctured, organ tissue may clog the holes and slow external bleeding. However, unlike a wound only to the stomach, which can result in little or no external blood, a liver wound should leave an obvious blood trail-, providing you do not push the animal, and you track it slowly and patiently.

I have found exceptional blood trails from some liver-shot deer, which resulted in sooner-than-anticipated recoveries. I assume this is because of a severed artery connecting to the liver. This small artery will not put a deer down as quick-ly as the three major arteries discussed in a later chapter. Nonetheless, I must believe that this artery, when severed, does have something to do with the amount of external blood that gets to the ground, and may put a liver-shot deer down soon-er than if the artery were not hit. Although I have not been able to locate and inspect this collapsed artery when field-dressing a liver-shot deer, it still seems likely that wounds to this artery have been responsible for some of my easiest liver-hit recov-eries.

If your arrow or projectile goes through more than one lobe of the liver, it may result in a better blood trail. Many times, after field dressing a liver-shot deer, I have discovered more than one hole. As mentioned previously, the lobes of the liver overlap. One could also assume that two holes in the liver may speed up death.

During the late archery season a few years ago, a doe approached within twenty-five yards of my stand and stood broadside. After passing several does early in the season, and now wanting to store away venison for the months ahead, I took aim and released an arrow. The arrow zipped through the deer quickly, but I could tell it hit her behind the diaphragm in the abdominal cavity. As the doe ran off, I watched her closely and assumed that I would be tracking a liver-shot or paunch-shot deer.

The doe ran parallel with my stand for about sixty yards, then turned and ran uphill. She angled up the hill for about thirty yards, then slowed up and stopped. Carefully, she dropped down and bedded. Thirty minutes after she bedded, the doe rolled onto her side and began thrashing. I knew it had ended.

Upon field dressing the doe, I found only a hole in the liver. The lungs and stomach had not been touched by my three-blade Muzzy broadhead. However, when I followed the blood trail back, I found an exceptional amount of blood on the right side of the trail (the side of the deer from which the arrow had exited). I could see another blood trail that came from the side of the deer where the arrow had entered, but it wasn't as obvious.

I have seen similar liver-shot deer leave blood trails like that one, and die within a shorter time than others. In those cases, I must believe that the small artery that connects to the liver was severed.

The blood trail of a liver-shot deer is normally steady when the deer walks. In some cases, the volume of external blood may increase after the deer travels about seventy-five yards. However, you will not find an exceptionally large amount of blood. Using persistence and patient tracking methods, you should recover the liver-shot deer within 250 yards, and oftentimes sooner, providing you do not push the deer.

I prefer to wait two or three hours before taking up the trail of a liver-shot deer. In some cases, a one-hour wait may do it, but it's better to be safe than sorry. It is common for a liver-shot deer to bed down within a short distance of where it was shot (providing it isn't aware of your presence). The last thing you would want to do is send it running from a bed.

Just how soon does a liver-shot deer bed down? Most seem to travel 100 to 150 yards. You could also find more than one bed. Many times, a liver-hit deer seems to get out of one bed and lie down again within a few yards. One deer I shot in the liver left seven beds before I found it in the eighth. In some cases, I have even found liver-shot deer expired, in a bedded posture.

Many years ago, my dad shot a doe just before dusk. He suspected a liver hit, and we waited about two hours before taking up the trail. Had we found any sign that the deer was paunch shot after we started trailing, we would have delayed the tracking even longer. However, all indications pointed to a liver wound. We were correct. We found the doe only eighty yards away, laying in a bed, in a bedded posture.

Stomach Wounds

In the previous section, I said it is better to deal with a liver wound than a stomach (rumen) or intestinal wound. If given the choice between a stomach wound or a wound to the intestines, however, I would much rather track a deer with a wound to the stomach.

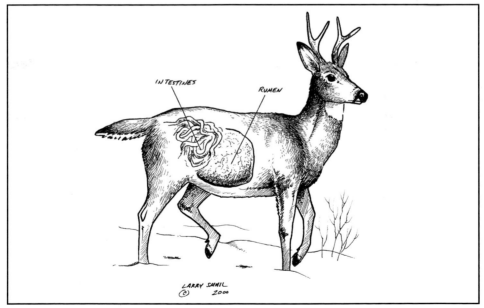

A deer hit in the stomach (rumen) will usually be easier to locate than a deer shot in the intestines.

Like the liver-shot deer, you should recover a stomach-shot deer. In fact, since 1987 I have had an excellent recovery rate. Many were not easily found, but persistence and the proper tracking techniques ultimately lead me to those stomach-shot deer.

In my first tracking book, Trailing Whitetails, published in 1987, I showed a table that provided the number of recoveries for various types of wounds. Some of these were deer I had shot with gun or bow; some were deer shot by others with gun or bow that I helped to track. Of fifty-seven paunch wounds, there were thirty-nine recoveries, for a success rate of sixty-eight percent. Those paunch wounds, however, consisted of both stomach and/or intestinal hits. The actual recovery rate of deer with only stomach wounds was probably much higher, assuming a few in that group were hit only in the intestines.

Since 1986, I have tracked twenty-two paunch-shot deer. Two were definitely hit in the intestines only. Of the twenty remaining deer, eighteen were hit in the stomach and recovered. Only one of those had to be shot again.

	Total Tracking Endeavors of Paunch-Shot Deer	Total Recoveries	Success Rate
1963 – 1986	57	39	68%
1987 – 1999	22	19	86%

Recovery rates of whitetail deer hit in the paunch (stomach and/or intestines only), up to and including 1986, and 1987 to 1999, as recorded by the author.

No doubt, in the past decade I've had an easier time recovering stomach-shot deer. I contribute my high percentage of recovery to a couple of things. As mentioned, I will not track a stomach-shot deer immediately, even if rain or snow threatens. I will wait several hours and take my chances, whereas, before the late 1980s, I went after a stomach-shot deer right away when bad weather threatened. Secondly, I am much more knowledgeable about stomach-shot deer today. I have researched this type of wound thoroughly, and have made it a point to learn all I can about the habits of a stomach-shot deer each time I track them.

Most hunters know that the deer is a ruminant, meaning it regurgitates its food. The regurgitation process is due to the deer's four-part stomach, and the deer chewing its cud. Each part of the stomach has its own compartment, and plays a role in the digestive process.

The stomach is quite large, and easily hit whenever a bullet or arrow hits about five to six inches behind the vital lungs. If the animal quarters into or away, the liver or intestines may also be punctured.

If you find hair from the middle of the deer's body, it will be very coarse, brown or gray with lighter tips than chest hair, and medium length. The hair from the bottom of the deer under the stomach will be white or light gray, coarse, slightly twisted, and long. If your arrow or projectile punches out the bottom of the deer, you should find hair at the location where the deer was shot.

The blood of the stomach-shot deer is dark red - lighter than the intestinal hit, but darker than a liver wound. You might determine the difference in a stomach and intestinal wound by examining the blood. The blood of a paunch-shot deer may have contents from the stomach or intestines. If hit in the stomach, the contents will be solid and usually light tan, whereas intestinal contents are runny, slimy, and dark brown or green. The contents may appear as only a fleck in a blood droplet. You may also find these contents when examining blood droplets in beds. In some cases, you can detect an odor on a spent arrow, or in a bed.

When hit in the stomach, a deer will not run hard, such as a deer hit in the lungs. It will often jump, take a few bounds, then stop if it doesn't know you are there. Some stomach-shot deer will only flinch, and then run gently for a short distance. However, when the deer moves away, it will usually walk slowly. The deer may also appear hunkered, with the back hunched and the legs widespread. You may also notice that the deer's neck and head are stretched out and even with the back - not above the back, as with an alert deer.

A gut-shot deer usually lunges forward, stops, then walks away. When it walks away, it appears hunkered with its head and neck lower than its back.

When certain of a stomach wound, I will wait four to six hours before tracking the deer, regardless of weather. Getting after a deer with a stomach wound right away makes no sense to me, even if the blood trail will soon be washed away. If I shoot a deer in the stomach during the evening, I put off the trailing until morning. If the shot takes place in the morning, I will usually wait until lunchtime. A stomach-shot deer bleeds very little anyway (exceptions do exist), and it will probably take a few hours for the animal to die. We also know that this deer will bed down promptly. Many times, if not pushed, it will die where it lies down.

Some stomach-shot deer lie in several beds, but most of the beds will be only a short distance apart. In other words, if you find a bed, more than likely the deer did not get up and move a hundred yards to another bed. It should bed down again within 20 to 40 yards of the first bed. For this reason, the tracker should watch ahead, and pay close attention to sounds that may signify the deer is up and moving. However, if you waited at least four to six hours before tracking the deer, it will probably be dead a short distance from the first bed you found.

Most stomach-shot deer will bed down after moving 100 to 150 yards. If you don't push it, you could find the deer lying in this bed, or another bed a short distance from the first one.

A year before I started to write this book, Vikki shot a doe at dusk. From the tree stand, she suspected that she hit the deer in the middle of the abdomen. After the doe walked out of sight, she waited for darkness, climbed down, and retrieved her arrow. After examining the arrow later that evening, I determined she had indeed hit the stomach.

We returned the next morning, found a few drops of blood, and tracked the deer for about fifty yards. Shortly thereafter, we lost the blood trail and widened the search, only to see the doe piled up about seventy-five yards ahead of the last blood droplet. She had died in the first place she laid.

My dad hit a small buck in the abdomen several years ago, in the same place that Vikki had hit with her doe. That buck traveled a little farther than the doe, and we found four beds, all within a sixty-yard circle. We recovered the buck in the fourth bed. Although most liver-shot deer will move away and out of sight before bedding down, you might see a stomach-shot deer lay right down. For this reason, watch the deer closely when it walks away. If it suddenly stops and stands in one place for a few minutes, it will probably lie down. If it does, sit tight and don't let the deer detect you. If darkness is approaching, wait until dark before leaving the area. If you shoot the deer in the morning, watch the deer and wait for it to make the next move. The last thing you want is to send a stomach-shot deer running or even walking away.

When tracking a stomach-shot deer, don't expect to find a large volume of blood. If your broadhead or bullet punches out on the bottom of the deer, you might find blood close to where you shot the deer, and perhaps at the shot location. If you hit the deer a few inches above the bottom, you may not find the first blood droplets until the deer has gone forty or fifty yards. The blood trail usually weakens, though, the farther you track the deer. This is due to organ tissue clogging the entry and/or departure hole. I have followed some stomach-shot deer that left respectable blood trails for about fifty or seventy-five yards, only to have them totally stop bleeding externally. When you do find a blood droplet, you may have to move several yards to find another. Sometimes, you may find only a fleck. If the deer stands in one location, you could find a circle of several blood droplets close together.

Some stomach-hit deer die sooner than others. Some also leave better blood trails. There are a couple of reasons for this, both of which the hunter can hope for. I asked Maltby if a bleeding spleen, or even a small severed artery feeding the stomach, would cause more bleeding and a quicker death.

"A bleeding spleen will cause the deer to bleed out much quicker than a wound to only the stomach," he told me. "If the mesenteric (pyloric) artery is hit, it would also cause the deer to bleed out sooner."

The pyloric artery comes off the aorta artery and branches off, connecting with organs in the abdominal cavity. If this semi-major artery is severed, you can assume it will speed up internal bleeding.

Since the spleen is small, many hunters do not notice it when field dressing a deer. The organ has a purplish-red color and lies just behind the diaphragm against the stomach. The spleen's task is to manufacture white blood cells, and filter foreign organisms and red blood cells.

A small percentage of stomach-shot deer may go to water. However, I've noticed this more when tracking deer with intestinal wounds. One small buck I tracked, bedded down after walking about 100 yards. I could not find any blood beyond the deer's bed. My son and I soon spread our search over a vast area, only to find the buck (six hours after the tracking started) lying slightly submerged in a pond. I soon discovered I had hit only the stomach. I have found other paunch-shot deer lying dead by creeks and small waterholes. I don't make a habit of searching for gut-shot deer near these areas, though, unless a blood trail expires and other attempts to recover the deer have failed.

Personally, I really don't mind tracking a deer hit in the stomach. I feel confident in recovering the deer, providing I wait long enough before trailing. However, it may be wise to get help before you begin. If you wait a few hours to start tracking, follow the trail slowly, and have a full understanding of the stomach-shot deer, your chances of a recovery are excellent.

The author has found that some gut-shot deer, particularly those that live for several hours, will go to water. Although dehydration will not be the cause of death, it may become a factor.

Intestinal Wounds

When judging the chances of recovering a liver-, stomach- or intestinal-shot deer, on a scale of one to ten -- with ten being the best chance of a recovery -- it is my opinion that those with intestinal wounds get a rating of two or three. Like the previously mentioned wounds, this deer will die. However, it may travel a long distance before bedding down, and it could take many hours for the deer to succumb. Additionally, the deer leaves a hard-to-follow blood trail, even if an arrow or projectile exits on the bottom of the animal.

The chance of hitting a deer in only the intestines is good if you hit too far back. There are about sixty-five feet of intestines in the deer, compacted into a large area in the back half of the body, behind the stomach to the hips. If I hit a deer too far back, I will hope for a high hit and a kidney wound.

The side hair of an intestinal wound is the same as the side wound of a stomach wound. The bottom or belly hair near the navel differs slightly from that of a stomach wound, however. It is coarse, white, long, and very curly. If your arrow or projectile punches out the bottom of the deer, more than likely you will find this white hair where the deer was standing when shot.

The darkest blood you will ever find when tracking a wounded deer comes from an intestinal wound. It is very dark red, and in some cases almost black. Seldom do you find blood at the location the deer stood when hit. Usually, the blood will not get to the ground until the deer has traveled at least fifty yards. This varies, though, depending upon the height of the entry or exit hole.

The reaction of the intestinal-shot deer is much like the stomach-shot deer.

It often appears hunched, and seldom leaves the scene running. If the deer runs, it appears sluggish, and will soon slow down and begin walking. If you can see at least fifty yards, you will probably notice this reaction, or see the deer stop and stand before it walks away out of view. One Illinois buck I shot low in the intestines simply lunged forward, walked about ten yards, and stood. In fact, he stood forty yards from my tree stand for about fifteen minutes. He then moved off into the thickets very slowly, with his back legs widespread. I'll discuss what hap-pened with this intestinal-shot buck in Chapter

Because of the difficulty in tracking a paunch-shot deer, it is best to have more than one individual participating. Organ tissue often clogs the entry and/or departure hole, preventing blood from getting to the ground.

You will often find less blood when you track an intestinal-shot deer than when you track a deer hit in the stomach. The holes in the deer seem to clog soon-er, perhaps because of the mushy tissue of the intestines, and the contents inside the intestines. I have seen some blood trails start well, but dwindle down to nothing in just a few yards. It's common to find only pin-sized drops of blood, even if the deer walks slowly or stands.

I commonly wait eight hours or more to begin tracking a deer with an intestinal wound. Most will not die as quickly, and most will travel farther than the stomach-shot deer before bedding. I have recovered some deer with intestinal wounds in six to eight hours, but have seen others live more than twenty-four hours. It is difficult to say why some live longer than others.

The bowhunter may find intestinal contents on an arrow shaft, and while the gun hunter or archer may find these contents in blood droplets or beds. Unlike stomach contents that have density, the contents of the intestines are usually runny and slimy to the touch. Intestinal contents are dark green, or dark brown. You may smell an odor when examining an arrow, blood, or bed, but the stench is not as rank as that which stems from a stomach wound.

One problem with recovering an intestinal-shot deer is the distance it travels before it beds down. Deer with liver and stomach wounds usually bed down within 100 to 150 yards of where they were shot. I recall one intestinal-shot deer that did not lie down until it traveled about a quarter mile. I had lost the blood trail earlier, and we had spread out our search, hoping to find a downed deer. As it was, we walked right up on the buck in its bed, still very much alive. Most deer with intestinal wounds will bed down within 200 to 300 yards of where they were shot. Exceptions do exist. I've seen some bed down only 100 to 150 yards away. Thus, it pays to look for beds. If you lose the blood trail and begin covering a wide area in search of sign, always look for beds and examine them closely for blood. The deer with an intestinal wound bleeds very little externally, but their bed will probably have at least some blood in it.

I once lost the trail of a deer with an intestinal wound after tracking the animal about 150 yards. Two hours later, Lady Luck helped me. I located a bed with only a few flecks of blood in it, about 200 yards from where I had lost the blood trail. I didn't find a blood trail leaving the bed, but my efforts still paid off. One hour later, while concentrating my search in the area of the bed, I found the deer about 100 yards away.

An intestinal wound, which leads to a loss of body fluids, could also cause dehydration. For this reason, look for a downed deer near water if you lose the blood trail. However, even though I have found that deer with intestinal wounds often go to water, Maltby said it is not dehydration that will kill the deer. Instead, it is internal bleeding, and a poisoning of the system due to the leakage of contents from the intestines. Nonetheless, because a deer with an intestinal wound may live for many hours, dehydration could become a factor in your recovery efforts.

Kidney Shot

A kidney wound should not be compared to other abdominal wounds, such as liver, spleen, stomach, and intestines. In fact, a deer with a kidney wound reacts much differently, and it dies quickly. It does not bed down, nor does internal bleeding take hours to kill the deer.

"Twenty-five percent of the blood goes to the kidneys all the time. If you hit a kidney, the deer is going to bleed to death real quick," noted Maltby.

There are two egg-shaped kidneys in the abdominal cavity of the deer, located under the spine in front of the hips. The kidneys of an adult deer are about three inches long by two inches wide. The hunter should not choose the small kidneys as a target, but if he hits a deer too far back, he can at least hope for a kidney wound. If your arrow or projectile hits the back portion of the abdominal cavity, one inch in any direction could make the difference in a deer going down in seconds (kidney wound) or many hours (intestinal wound).

Deer with abdominal wounds (other than kidneys) usually seek dense cover and bed down. If blood is not getting to the ground, look for beds nearby. (Photo by Vikki L. Trout.)

The kidneys extract waste products from the blood with filtering units. The metabolic waste is then transported to the bladder for excretion. The blood that flows to the kidneys is delivered by the renal artery, which comes from the major aorta artery. Thus, a wound to a kidney will cause rapid hemorrhage. In fact, a physician and surgeon I talked with many years ago told me that a hole in the kidneys could be compared to removing the drain plug in a bathtub.

The hair of a kidney wound resembles that of other high-hit abdominal wounds, except it is slightly shorter. The hair is very coarse, dark brown or gray with black tips, and about two and a half inches long. You seldom find hair on the ground where the deer stood when shot, but you could find hair on an arrow that has passed through the deer.

If you hit the kidneys, expect to find crimson-red blood, similar to that of a heart shot. The blood trail usually begins within ten to fifteen yards. In some cases, you might find blood at the hit location. A kidney-shot deer often jumps straight up, then begins running hard, but not as hard as a deer hit in both lungs. The running pace will slow after thirty or forty yards, or the deer may begin walking and staggering. Most kidney-shot deer drop in less than 100 yards. Of the kidney-shot deer I have tracked, some traveled no more than fifty yards, and none traveled farther than seventy-five yards.

Even if an arrow or bullet angles downward and hits the intestines along with the kidneys, the deer will bleed externally and provide the hunter with an easy-to-see blood trail. However, the blood trail is not as profound as that of a major artery wound. The blood may spurt to the sides of the trail a few feet, but much of the hemorrhage is internal.

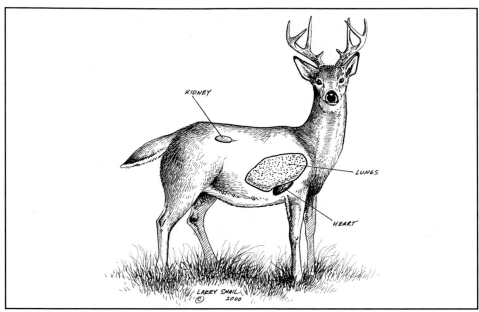

Unlike most abdominal wounds, a kidney-shot deer goes down quickly, due to rapid hemorrhaging.

Many hunters are never aware that they have hit the kidneys. A bowhunter may see the arrow enter the back portion of the abdominal cavity, but would have no idea if it hit the kidneys unless he can accurately read the blood trail. If I hit too far back in the deer, I will examine the color of blood carefully, and the amount of blood on the ground. If it looks like the animal is only gut shot (dark blood), I will delay tracking the animal as necessary. However, if I find bright blood, I will track the deer immediately.

Since the kidneys are small, they often go unnoticed even when field dressing the animal. If a broadhead or projectile does not mutilate the kidneys, you will notice they are hard to the touch, and often engulfed in a layer of fat.

© **Ted Rose**

Chapter 9

Artery Wounds

There are numerous blood vessels in the deer's body. This chapter will focus on three primary arteries: carotid, aorta (sometimes called aortic), and femoral. When severed, each of these arteries will cause a quick death. However, the blood trail, the deer's reaction, and the tracking endeavor will differ, depending upon the artery your broadhead or bullet hits.

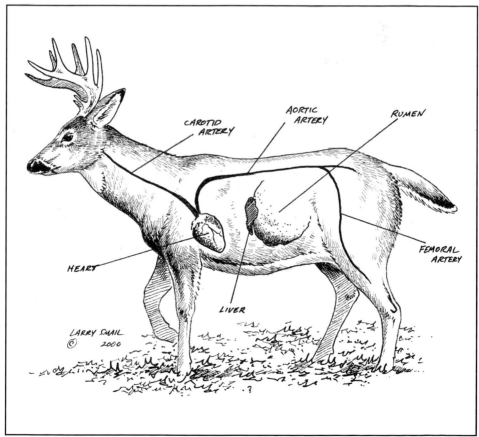

There are three major arteries in the deer's body. Rapid death occurs when the aorta, carotid, or femoral artery is severed.

There are smaller arteries and veins that will cause blood loss, and oftentimes death. Previously, you read about a couple of the secondary arteries that connect to organs (liver and stomach) in the abdominal cavity. When severed, secondary arteries will not bleed as profusely as the three major arteries, simply because they donít carry as much blood.

A deer must lose about one-third of its blood before it bleeds to death. We also know that a deer has about one ounce of blood per pound of body weight. Thus, you can safely assume that a 150-pound deer must lose about fifty ounces (3.125 pints) of blood before it succumbs. However, it is likely that a deer will go in to shock before losing that much blood.

It should be understood that blood goes a long way when spread out into droplets on the ground. To give you an example of how far blood goes, I have, in the past, bottled up blood from a freshly killed deer to use for photos. While staging the tracking photos, I place a few drops of blood about three feet apart for a distance of fifty yards. The mock blood trail resembles that of a wounded deer bleeding steadily, yet it takes only about one ounce of blood to make the trail. Each hunter should consider this fact if following a steady trail of blood droplets for 300 yards. It may seem as if the deer has lost a lot of blood, but in reality the animal has probably lost less than ten ounces.

When hunters follow an easy-to-see blood trail, they often believe they have severed an artery. While it may be true that a lot of external blood could indicate an artery wound, it could only be a muscle wound, long scrape wound, or a severed minor blood vessel. That's not to say that a deer with a severe muscle wound cannot be recovered. On the contrary, you might be able to recover a deer that bleeds profusely, even though a major artery hasn't been severed. However, the hunter should not, as the old saying goes, "judge a book by its cover." If there is profuse bleeding and you find a lot of external blood, though, you can at least hope for a severed major artery.

As a deer bleeds to death, its body temperature rapidly declines and it goes into shock. Although many wounds may cause shock, an artery wound will speed up the process, simply because the blood pours out so quickly. Medical science has also determined that shock causes numbness. Therefore, a severed major artery probably results in a fast and painless death.

Aorta Artery

The aorta artery stems from the heart and travels up to and under the deer's spine, practically the entire length of the body. It branches off into smaller arteries, which feed blood to some organs in the abdomen.

A wound to the lungs, or the upper portion of the heart, might also result in a wound to the aorta artery. This severed artery usually goes unnoticed by the hunter, even when field dressing the animal. However, I have tracked several deer that were hit by a bullet or broadhead under the spine that resulted in a wound to muscle and the aorta artery. The lungs and heart of these animals were spared, but those deer went down within 100 to 150 yards due to the severed aorta artery.

Back hair under the spine is brown or gray with black tips, very coarse, hollow, and long. However, it is shorter than hair that comes from the top of the deer's back.

You can expect to find bright-red blood, although it may be pinkish if you also hit the lungs. A high hit and a severed aorta artery may not get blood to the ground until the animal has run twenty to thirty yards. The deer will bleed profusely, internally and externally, and will usually run hard after being hit. Their run is similar to that of a deer hit in only the loin, except the deer will not travel far. The blood often spurts a foot or more to the sides of the deer's tracks when the aorta artery is severed, whereas, when you hit only the loin, the blood lands within inches of the tracks. However, blood does not spurt to the sides of the trail as far as from deer with wounds to the carotid or femoral artery. I have also seen deer with a severed aorta artery run erratically, similar to that of a heart-shot deer.

Blood will often spurt to the sides of the trail if a major artery is severed. However, because a similar, profuse blood loss may occur externally after other types of wounds, always track the deer patiently and quietly.

Determining whether you hit the aorta artery is a difficult task. Any collapsed artery is difficult to locate when field dressing the animal. If you do hit a deer about four inches below the back, recover it within a short distance and determine you missed the lungs, you can safely assume your broadhead or projectile severed the aorta artery.

High body hits often result in superficial wounds. In fact, hunters commonly dread seeing a wound in the back of a deer, simply because they have less chance of a recovery if they miss the aorta artery. However, some hunters are unexpectedly rewarded after hitting a deer in the back and severing the aorta artery.

Carotid Artery and Jugular Vein

The carotid artery travels through the neck of a deer and delivers blood to the brain. At one time, I believed it to be the same blood vessel as the jugular vein. However, the jugular vein is an entirely different blood vessel, and runs alongside the carotid artery. The carotid artery delivers blood from the heart to the brain, while the jugular takes blood from the brain to the heart. Damage to either blood vessel results in a quick death. The deer suffers rapid blood loss, and will lose consciousness and die within seconds.

If your bullet or projectile severs the carotid artery or jugular vein, the blood loss is primarily external. Thus, the hunter will have an easy-to-follow blood trail. The bright-red blood is often found at the shot location, or within a few yards of where you hit the deer. You often find blood that spurts up to two feet away from the sides of the trail, unlike a muscle wound in the neck that leaves blood closer to the deer's trail, or even in the tracks of a walking deer.

The hunter often finds short neck hairs (1.5 to 1.75 inches) where the deer was shot. Bullet wounds to the neck almost always leave hair on the ground, but even an arrow wound may result in hair on the ground. Neck hair is thin and light gray. You may also find white hair if the bullet or broadhead exits on the underside of the neck.

When the carotid artery or jugular vein is severed, the animal usually bolts, runs hard, and goes down within 100 yards. However, I know of one that traveled only forty yards. I have never seen a deer travel more than 125 yards after the carotid artery or jugular vein was severed.

Despite the killing power of a severed carotid artery or jugular vein, the neck should not be a target. These blood vessels, as well as the other neck vitals that can kill quickly, such as the windpipe and vertebrate, are small. In fact, a wound to the neck is much more likely to result in only a muscle wound, and a difficult deer to recover.

Femoral Artery

Some hunters hope they have hit the femoral artery while tracking a ham-shot deer. Nobody enjoys rolling into a check station with a deer that has a hole in its rump. However, a quick recovery is in store if you are fortunate enough to hit one of the femoral arteries.

The femoral arteries branch off the aorta artery at the hip of the deer, and travel down each hind leg to the Achilles' tendon. The femoral arteries are seldom severed when a hunter shoots at a deer quartering to him, however. Usually, the broadhead or bullet will hit the artery only if the animal is broadside, or is quartering away. The best possibility of hitting it occurs when the deer is facing away, since the artery is closer to the outside of the rump. To reach the artery when a deer is standing broadside, the arrow or bullet must go through the heavy muscle in the ham, and shatter the leg bone (femur). Nonetheless, a hip shot is not a shot that any hunter should take intentionally.

When a major artery is hit, the deer usually runs hard. One exception could occur when the femoral artery is hit, since there will also be damage to muscles in the ham, and sometimes in the leg bone.

Like a hit to the neck, a ham shot may result in hair found at the location where the deer was hit. The hair from the hip is coarse, and gray with dark tips. It is shorter than chest hair but longer than lower leg hair.

If you sever the femoral artery, you can expect to find bright-red blood close to the site where the deer was hit. Although a deer hit in the ham and femoral artery may run hard, its motivation could be altered. A broken bone, as well as severed muscles, may cause the deer to have a problem using its leg. I've seen deer run perfectly up to about twenty-five yards, only to begin having problems after that.

Most deer with a severed femoral artery will go down in less than 100 yards. If I track a hip-shot deer and do not find the animal within 150 yards, I assume that I missed the femoral artery. An exception is a low hit. The femoral artery narrows as it travels down the leg. If the low, narrow portion of the artery is severed, bleeding is steady but not as profuse. Thus, the deer may travel slightly farther than one that is hit high in the ham. However, even if the femoral artery is spared, a wound to only hip muscles can put a deer down. As you will read in the following chapter, most ham wounds will result in a recovery when the hunter uses the proper tracking techniques.

The first time I followed the trail of a deer hit in the femoral artery, I was amazed with the blood trail. I found blood only on one side of the deer's trail, but the wound bled profusely and often sprayed out a few feet to the sides of the trail. Many muscle wounds start this way, but the blood trail will taper after the deer starts walking. We recovered this buck in less than seventy-five yards. Since that day, I have helped to track several deer hit in the femoral artery. Each of the blood trails was similar to this one.

You may find blood in the deer's tracks if the animal travels more than seventy-five yards. This is caused by blood running down the animal's leg. The farther it travels with a severed femoral artery, the better the chance of finding blood in the tracks. With any hip wound, you could find blood in tracks, but many deer hit in the femoral artery go down before the blood has a chance to run down the entire length of the leg.

Summary

Bright-red or crimson blood calls for immediate tracking. Even if an artery is not severed, and you have hit only muscles, you will be doing the right thing by pursuing the animal within twenty minutes of the time it was shot. Interestingly, the reactions of a deer will differ, depending upon the major artery that was severed. The result is the same, in that a wound to any of the three major arteries will result in a quick death to the deer. However, I would suggest that you never take for granted that you hit a major artery when tracking a wounded deer. By doing so, you may hurry and push a deer farther away. Always remember that there are numerous blood vessels in a deer, some of which will cause profuse external bleeding similar to what you will find when tracking a deer with a severed major artery.

Chapter 10

Muscular and Skeletal Wounds

    Oftentimes, we must track a deer that has received a wound to muscle, bone, or both. In many cases, our arrow or projectile has not penetrated the body cavity and the wound is superficial. However, you do have a chance of recovering a deer that has a skeletal or muscular wound if you use the proper tracking techniques. In some cases, slowly pushing a deer with a superficial wound will put the animal down, or provide a second shot.

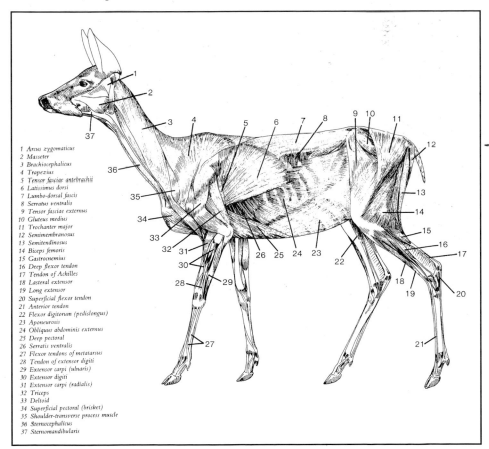

1 Arcus zygomaticus
2 Masseter
3 Brachiocephalicus
4 Trapezius
5 Tensor fasciae antebrachii
6 Latissimus dorsi
7 Lumbo-dorsal fascis
8 Serratus ventralis
9 Tensor fasciae externus
10 Gluteus medius
11 Trochanter major
12 Semimembranosus
13 Semitendinosus
14 Biceps femoris
15 Gastrocnemius
16 Deep flexor tendon
17 Tendon of Achilles
18 Lateral extensor
19 Long extensor
20 Superficial flexor tendon
21 Anterior tendon
22 Flexor digitorum (pedislongus)
23 Aponeurosis
24 Obliquus abdominis externus
25 Deep pectoral
26 Serratis ventralis
27 Flexor tendons of metatarsus
28 Tendon of extensor digiti
29 Extensor carpi (ulnaris)
30 Extensor digiti
31 Extensor carpi (radialis)
32 Triceps
33 Deltoid
34 Superficial pectoral (brisket)
35 Shoulder-transverse process muscle
36 Sternocephalicus
37 Sternomandibularis

Muscular system (Illustration by Robert Pratt and Wayne Trimm. Courtesy of Wildlife Management Institute.)

Let me emphasize the importance of tracking a deer with only a muscular or skeletal wound. Regardless of how trivial the wound may appear, you should always put forth your best effort into tracking that animal. In fact, an ethical hunter will apply as much effort into locating a superficially wounded deer as he will with one that is hit in the body cavity. Give up the trail only when the blood trail expires, and after you have done everything possible to locate the deer. More than once I have recovered deer with seemingly insignificant wounds, simply because I refused to quit.

After shooting a deer in a non-vital area, your best chance of recovery will depend upon your understanding of the wound. Sometimes, blood loss will be the deciding factor; sometimes, severe muscle or bone damage will make it possible for you to get up on and shoot the deer again; sometimes the severity of the wound will cause the animal to go into shock. For these reasons, I would suggest you track a deer with a muscular or skeletal wound immediately. That is, providing you are certain that your arrow or bullet did not enter the abdominal cavity, before or after it hits muscle or bone. Here's a look at the muscular and skeletal wounds you may have to deal with.

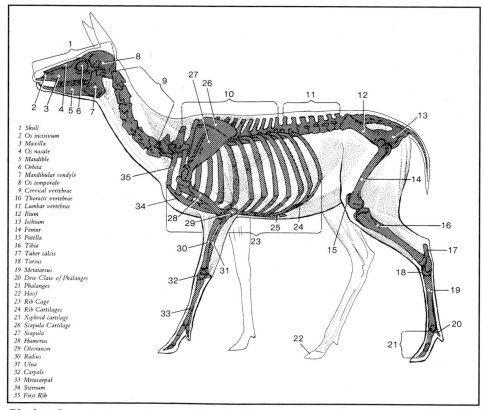

1 Skull
2 Os incisivum
3 Maxilla
4 Os nasale
5 Mandible
6 Orbita
7 Mandibular condyle
8 Os temporale
9 Cervical vertebrae
10 Thoracic vertebrae
11 Lumbar vertebrae
12 Ilium
13 Ischium
14 Femur
15 Patella
16 Tibia
17 Tuber calcis
18 Tarsus
19 Metatarsus
20 Dew Claw of Phalanges
21 Phalanges
22 Hoof
23 Rib Cage
24 Rib Cartilages
25 Xiphoid cartilage
26 Scapula Cartilage
27 Scapula
28 Humerus
29 Olecranon
30 Radius
31 Ulna
32 Carpals
33 Metacarpal
34 Sternum
35 First Rib

Skeletal system (Illustration by Robert Pratt and Wayne Trimm. Courtesy of Wildlife Management Institute.)

Back and Loin Wounds

There are three types of back wounds: spine, loin, and high back shots. Any of these wounds could also result in a severed aorta artery, depending upon the angle of the shot. However, I will focus on those back wounds that do not include a severed aorta artery.

Spine shots are welcome sights because a deer will drop immediately. When a broadhead or bullet severs the spine, the deer becomes immobilized. The precise location of the severed spine will determine how much mobility the deer has. I have seen some spine-shot deer that were able to crawl, while others could not.

If the forward portion of the spine above the shoulder is severed, the deer may be completely immobilized. However, if the wound occurs in the middle of the deer, or near the hips, the deer may still have use of its front legs. If this is the case, you may have to shoot the deer again. If you shoot a deer and it appears to have lost some mobility, approach the deer carefully and make certain you place your second shot through the lungs. Otherwise, a spine-shot deer might not succumb for a long time. Following up with a second shot is always the ethical thing to do.

Back wounds result in crimson-red blood. Hair from the top of the deer's back is very coarse, hollow, long, and dark gray with black tips. There is little difference in the hair by the loin, except that it is slightly longer. If the deer drops immediately, you might find hair at the shot location.

A deer with a wound to the top of the back - above the spine - will probably recover. In fact, I have never recovered a deer that was hit on top of the back, except for one that gave me a second shot.

Bowhunters may determine they hit the top of the back by examining their arrow for tallow. Tallow is found along the top of the deer's back near the spine but close to the hips, and on the brisket of the deer.

Because the hit is on top of the deer's body, you will find little if any blood on the ground at the shot location - that is, providing the deer does not drop immediately. Even if a broadhead or projectile slices a wide gash across the top of the deer's back, the hide will usually soak up the blood and keep most of it from getting to the ground.

A shot in the loin seldom results in a downed deer either, but the possibility of a recovery does increase slightly when compared to a deer with a wound to the top of the back.

The loin is a narrow strip of muscle (about ten inches long) in the back half of the deer. It lies under the spine, above the kidneys.

A deer hit in the loin will usually bolt and run hard, similar to what a lung-shot deer will do. After running about 100 yards, it will usually slow and begin walking. Many loin-shot deer will bed down after the initial run, or shortly thereafter. However, to recover the deer, you will probably have to shoot it again. That is providing you can get close enough for a shot. Obviously, the gun hunter will have a much better chance of getting a second shot than the bowhunter.

**A loin-shot deer will often bed down after travel-
ing 150 to 200 yards from the shot location.
However, the wound usually proves to be superficial unless the hunter can get close enough for a
second shot.**

If you suspect a loin hit, follow the blood trail very slowly and watch ahead
of you for a moving deer. Some loin-shot deer will move slow, stop occasionally,
and watch their backtrail. Shoot again only if you can positively identify your target as the wounded deer.

I have found that most deer hit in the loin with an arrow leave a better blood
trail than those hit with a bullet. With either weapon, though, blood will probably
not get to the ground until the deer has run about thirty to forty yards. It's also common for the blood trail to increase after the animal slows to a walk and has traveled
about 100 yards. While this may inspire the tracker, it usually provides false hope.

After the deer travels about 150 yards, the blood trail will begin to diminish. A deer with a loin hit is not likely to die from blood loss.

One last thing should be mentioned about back wounds. Don't be fooled when a deer is hit in the back and drops to the ground. Some back-shot deer will drop immediately, even if you miss the spine. One buck I hit with an arrow dropped and thrashed around for better than sixty seconds, only to get up and run away. I never recovered that deer.

Who knows why a back wound will cause some deer to drop immediately when the spine is not severed? It may be due to nerve damage, and in some cases the deer may go into temporary shock due to excessive trauma. However, always be prepared to shoot a back-hit deer again, even when it appears as if the animal is not going anywhere.

Brisket Wounds

I briefly discussed the brisket wound in Chapter 7. The brisket lies under the heart, and is often hit if the shot is low or angled downward. I don't believe it is possible to recover a deer that receives only a brisket wound, unless a broadhead or bullet makes a long gash across the bottom of the deer.

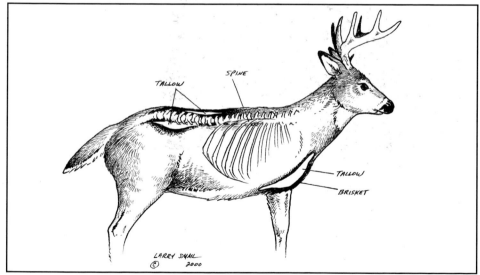

If an arrow or bullet passes through the brisket, the tracker may find tallow. Tallow is thick in three areas of the deer's body, but the largest portion is located in the brisket. Northern deer tend to have more tallow than southern deer.

This will increase the amount of blood that gets to the ground, allow you to follow the deer farther, and perhaps get another shot.

A gun hunter may not realize he has hit the brisket unless he is lucky enough to find specks of tallow in the blood droplets on the ground. The bowhunter, if he retrieves his spent arrow (he probably will if he only hit the brisket) should find tallow on the arrow shaft or vanes. Tallow is difficult to see on feathers, and is seldom found on the broadhead.

When checking an arrow for tallow, run your fingers across the shaft. Tallow is off-white, sticky, and gummy.

The largest portion of tallow is found in the deer's brisket. As mentioned previously, there is also a small section of tallow near the deer's spine. Tallow has an off-white color, is greasy and somewhat sticky. The best way to find tallow on an arrow is to view it under a bright light, or run your fingers across the shaft.

When an arrow enters a deer high on the chest and exits through the bottom of the brisket, you might find more tallow than blood on the shaft. This occurs because some of the blood on the shaft is cleaned off as it passes through the brisket. It also is possible you will find blood only on one side of the shaft.

A brisket wound results in crimson-red blood. You might find blood at the shot location, although there may be little blood on the arrow that passes through the brisket. Hair may also be found at the shot location. Brisket hair is dark brown or gray with black tips, and is long and stiff.

When you follow the blood trail of a brisket-shot deer, it will usually begin diminishing after the deer has traveled about fifty yards or so. If the blood trail intensifies, more than likely the path of your arrow or bullet was high enough to hit the heart. A typical brisket wound will bleed for 100 to 150 yards before the wound begins to coagulate. The amount of blood on the ground will be determined by the hole in the brisket. A long gash across the brisket will result in more external blood loss. However, as the blood trail subsides, you may find only pin-sized drops of blood. Few deer with brisket wounds will bed down.

Ham Wounds

If you read the previous chapter, you are aware of the femoral arteries and their location in each hip. A severed femoral artery is the best thing to hope for when a hip wound occurs, but a wound only to the ham can still result in a recovery. A hip wound always results in a severe wound to heavy muscle, and sometimes the femur or hip bones are broken. However, if your broadhead or bullet penetrates only muscle, you still have an excellent chance of finding the deer. Sometimes, a second shot is necessary.

Deer shot in the hams are often recovered, even if the femoral artery is spared. Because of severe muscle damage, a patient tracker will usually get close enough for a second shot, or he can push the deer until blood loss causes the animal to succumb.

It's not much fun hitting a deer in the ham, since it indicates your shot was way off target (providing the animal was broadside when you shot). However, it does happen occasionally. I don't go for the idea of shooting at a deer running straight away, but the fact remains that the ham shot is deadly.

If you do hit the ham of the deer, odds are you will not hit the femoral artery. Thus, you can safely assume you will be tracking a deer with a muscular wound, or perhaps one with a broken bone and a muscular wound. A deer may have problems moving with one broken femur, but it can still do so. On the other hand, it usually has problems when the damage is to muscle only. The muscle damage also causes major blood loss, and an easy to follow trail. Of course, the more the arrow or projectile penetrates the muscle, the better damage that occurs and the better chance you have of recovering the deer.

You will find bright-red blood when you hit the ham. If the deer angles toward you or away from you when you shoot, you could also hit the abdominal cavity, and find both bright and dark-colored blood.

You will seldom find hair at the shot location after hitting a deer in the ham. However, you may find hair on an arrow if it breaks off along the trail, or find hair in the deer's bed. Ham hair is very coarse, about two inches long (longer than lower leg hair), dark brown or gray with black tips. A deer hit in the ham will usually tear away fast from the shot location. It will run hard for thirty to fifty yards, then begin to slow down. It will bleed very well externally, and you should find blood close to the shot location, even if the hit is high in the ham.

After the deer travels a short distance, the blood trail will intensify. If mobility is a problem, the blood trail will be easier to follow. When tracking a ham-shot deer, look for scuffed leaves and marks in the soil. If the deer has a problem using one of its back legs, there will be obvious sign on the ground.

Although I have seen some ham-shot deer travel 200 yards or more before bedding, most will bed down within 150 yards. I shot one that traveled only sixty yards before bedding. My arrow hit only muscle, but the wound was quite severe. I watched the deer for about fifteen minutes, then climbed down from my tree stand. The deer watched as I approached, but allowed me to get within twenty yards. A second arrow ended the ordeal. I was not proud of this experience, but it was the ethical thing to do.

Severe hemorrhage occurs when your arrow or projectile hits the ham of a deer. Although the blood loss could cause the animal to succumb, any major blood loss may cause shock. If the deer runs, blood may spurt to one side of the trail. When it walks, or after it has run about seventy-five yards, you will probably find blood in the tracks.

Always follow the blood trail cautiously and be on the lookout for the deer up ahead. You may hear it getting out of its bed, or see or hear the animal moving up ahead. The gun hunter should have no problem locating the animal and getting another shot, but even a bowhunter has an excellent chance of getting up close to a ham-shot deer and shooting it again.

Over the years, I have tracked many ham-shot deer that were not hit in the femoral artery. I recovered most of them. I attribute this success to immediate pursuit, easy-to-see blood trails, and having a good understanding of the ham wound.

Head Wounds

You may never find yourself tracking a deer with a head wound, but the possibility always exists that somehow an arrow or projectile will be off target and hit the head. If this occurs, the deer will either drop immediately or receive only a superficial wound.

If a broadhead or bullet hits the brain, the deer will go down and remain motionless. I have never seen, or heard of a brain-shot deer that thrashed violently, although severe trauma can occur when a bullet hits the antlers of a buck, which could make you think the brain was hit.

Many years ago, my dad shot a huge buck at dawn, moments after legal shooting time. The deer was on a hill about sixty yards away, but heavy foliage surrounding the animal made it difficult to see him well. After determining the animal was standing broadside, he settled his sights just behind the buck's shoulder and squeezed the trigger of his slugster. However, just when Dad shot, he recalled seeing the buck's head move. No problem, he thought, as the deer dropped to the ground immediately after the shot.

At first Dad stayed put and watched the motionless buck. Once he believed the animal was down to stay, he slowly approached, prematurely congratulating himself for the kill. However, when he got within twenty-five yards of the buck, it suddenly began thrashing. The deer then sprang to its feet and took off over the hill before Dad could get off another shot.

Unsure what had happened, but assuming he had hit the shoulder, he looked for blood on the ground. To his surprise, he found a large section of the buck's left antler that had been neatly whacked off by the twelve-gauge slug. Apparently, the blow to the deer's antler had momentarily knocked him uncon-scious for a few second. Dad assumed the deer had moved its head back onto its shoulder the moment he squeezed the trigger, to look at his backtrail. The slug probably sailed a little high, hitting the antler and causing the buck to drop. Dad did look for blood, just in case the slug had hit the deer's body, but after a long and determined search that revealed nothing, finally decided the buck received only a headache and an education.

Of the two head-shot deer I have tracked, I found bright-red blood in both cases. However, the blood trails were sparse and both trails expired in less than 100 yards. I have to believe that a head shot will result in a downed deer only if the deer's brain is hit, or if the deer is knocked to the ground and the hunter makes a well-placed second shot.

Leg Wounds

Obviously, leg wounds occur when a hunter shoots low. Deer that receive wounds to two legs are usually recovered. In fact, those deer cannot maneuver at all. Tracking a deer with a wound to only one leg, however, can become a long and frustrating adventure. Surprisingly, many hunters do recover these deer.

When an arrow hits a leg and breaks bone, the bowhunter will usually hear a loud crack, unlike the dull thump heard when an arrow hits ribs. Like most muscular and skeletal wounds, a leg wound will result in bright-red blood, often found at the shot location. Hair is often found at the precise location, particularly if the wound is only an inch or two above or below the knee. The hair of the lower leg is very coarse, dark gray or brown, and only about one and a half inches long.

If bone is not broken when the bullet or broadhead hits the leg, the deer will run hard. If bone is broken, the deer may appear clumsy when it leaves the scene. However, I have heard stories about mature bucks that have run very well with one broken leg.

Hunters should also be aware of the Achilles' tendon, located under the hams of each back leg behind the tibia. If the Achilles' tendon is severed, the deer will have problems motivating. However, it can still run. Bleeding however, may be excessive since the femoral artery runs through the tendon. The artery narrows after leaving the hams, and will not bleed as profusely as a severed artery in the ham, but nonetheless it will result in a downed deer.

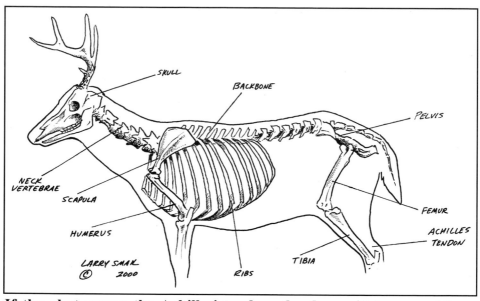

If the shot severs the Achilles' tendon, the deer will have problems motivating. The femoral artery may also be severed.

The blood trail of a leg-shot deer is often intense for the first 100 yards, and then begins to decrease. Eventually, you will find blood in the deer's tracks. You might also find fragments of bone. Many leg-shot deer will bed down after moving 150 yards. If the deer is in a bed for an hour or two, coagulation begins and the blood trail going away from the bed will be more difficult to follow.

You might find drag marks when following a deer with a broken leg. However, I believe there is a far better chance of a deer dragging a hoof if a back leg is broken. Drag marks will show up best in snow or sandy soil. If you track a leg-shot deer through heavy leaves, you will probably see scuffed marks where the leg has dragged.

It's not unusual to find a drag mark if the deer's leg is broken. (Photo by Vikki L. Trout.)

As with the ham-shot deer, the leg-shot deer can be recovered if the hunter can get close enough for a second shot. Many young deer with leg wounds seem to bed down quickly and stay in the bed longer than mature deer when they see a hunter approach.

Although the blood trail of a leg-shot deer may decrease after a short distance, it will often remain steady enough to follow if the hunter tracks the deer cautiously and quietly. Some hunters have followed the trail of leg-shot deer for miles.

One year on Thanksgiving morning, I shot a respectable eight-pointer as he pursued a doe. My slug hit the deer low in the right front leg, and he had no problem leaving the scene rapidly. I slowly trailed the buck for the next three hours, finally jumping him from a bed in a pine thicket about 200 yards from where I shot him. I could not find any more blood, so I called off the tracking episode, went home, and did my best to enjoy dinner.

Despite everyone's appeal to stay home the rest of the day, I returned to the woods, hoping to pick up the trail of the wounded buck. About one hour after I widened my search from the buck's bed, I found more blood. The moving deer began bleeding steadily, and although the droplets had dried, they were easy to see. I followed the trail for another hour, only to come across a place where the buck had stood for a long time. Blood covered a fifteen-yard circle of ground. This time, though, I found wet blood and assumed the deer may have seen me coming.

Just before dusk, moving ever so carefully along the sparse blood trail, I spotted a deer with antlers walking slowly about fifty yards in front of me in a dense stand of hardwoods. I shouldered the gun, but couldn't tell if it was the same buck that I shot that morning. Needless to say, I couldn't shoot. With darkness only moments away, I could only mark the spot where I saw the moving deer.

The next morning, I found blood where I had seen the deer moving the previous evening. I then knew it was the buck I had shot. So, I got back on the trail and followed the deer for another 150 yards, only to lose the trail for good. A determined search of the area in the hours that followed proved futile. Although this leg-shot buck was not recovered, there are many stories of others that were found by hunters that did not give up the trail. Persistence is the key when tracking a leg-shot deer. Fortunately, an obvious blood trail usually helps a persistent hunter to track the animal slowly and quietly for a long distance.

A leg-shot deer can sometimes be followed for miles. Persistent tracking will increase your chances of a recovery.

Neck Wounds

A deer's neck contains major blood vessels, the windpipe, and the vertebrate, all of which will put a deer down quickly when severed. Surprisingly, though, your broadhead or bullet can rip through the neck and easily miss these vitals. In fact, if you do hit the neck, more than likely your arrow or projectile will hit above or below the vitals, and you will be dealing with only a muscle wound.

If you hit the vertebrate in the neck, the deer will drop to the ground immediately, as it does when the spine is broken. The deer will have no mobility and will only slightly quiver. However, some deer will drop to the ground when a projectile passes though the neck, even if it misses the vertebrate. But this deer will usually get back on its feet quickly and run away.

When a deer receives severe damage to neck muscles, its head might appear slumped, and low to the ground when it runs away. One buck that I remember, after running forty yards and slowing up to a walk, had his head about six inches off the ground. Each time the deer took a step, his head swayed from side-to-side.

Although the broadhead or bullet misses the vitals in the neck, severed muscles in the neck might cause the deer's head to lower as it runs away.

Neck hair is often found at the shot location, or on a spent arrow. The hair is dark brown or gray, has black tips, and is shorter than the deer's body hair. If the deer beds down, you might also find hair in its bed.

You can expect to find bright-red blood when neck muscles are severed. The blood will usually get to the ground within twenty to thirty yards of where the animal was shot. Blood is often found close to the center of the trail, and seldom to the sides when the deer walks. The blood will spurt out farther from the center of the trail when the deer runs, and the blood trail will intensify slowly as you track the deer. Many times, I find more blood on the ground after tracking a neck-shot deer more than 100 yards. After the deer has traveled more than 200 yards, however, the blood trail weakens.

Most of the bleeding that occurs is external, and the severity of the wound will play a role in how far you can track the deer. If you pass through the neck completely, and there is both an entry and exit hole, for example, odds are you will track the deer farther than you would if the deer has only one hole. I know of some neck-shot deer that hunters tracked for less than half a mile. Personally, I once followed the trail of one neck-shot buck for more than a mile.

A neck-shot deer may bed down after traveling 150 to 200 yards. However, many do not. One thing I have noticed is that they will sometimes stand in a given spot for a long time. Oftentimes, when following the trail of a neck-shot deer, I come across two or three locations with large circles of blood. This indicates the deer stood for a long time in each spot.

What are your chances of recovering a neck-shot deer when the vitals are spared? Not good. Although it may bleed profusely, it probably will not die of blood loss. However, you can often track a neck-shot easily, thanks to the profuse bleeding that normally occurs. As is with other muscular wounds, you should get on the trail immediately and follow the trail slowly and quietly, watching ahead at all times for the wounded deer. Your best chance of a recovery is to prevent coagulation. If you keep the deer walking slowly, it will continue to bleed, allowing you to stay on the trail.

Shoulder Wounds

When a bullet hits and breaks the scapula (shoulder blade), the deer will often drop to the ground immediately, or at least to its front knees. Moments later, it may get up and run away. If a broadhead or projectile hits and breaks the scapula in both shoulders, the animal will not get up and run away. It will usually stay down and thrash violently for a few seconds, eventually succumbing because both lungs are also hit. Exceptions do exist.

Bowhunters have always feared the shoulder, knowing it can stop a swift-moving, heavy arrow. Today's modern archery equipment has reduced this possibility, but it still happens. However, I'm a firm believer that the scapula does not stop as many arrows as the joint that lies between the scapula and the humerus. Actually, the scapula breaks easily when hit, and often allows the arrow to continue forward into the lungs. The joint, on the other hand, is extremely thick and capable of stopping an arrow, and in some cases deflecting or shattering a bullet. The joint is forward in the deer's shoulder, and a little closer to the bottom than the top of the deer. I have come to believe this theory after seeing broadheads embedded in the joint, and after seeing them work out of the deer after it runs a short distance. Interestingly, I have found fewer broadheads embedded in the scapula.

The problem with the joint or scapula stopping a broadhead or bullet is penetration. The arrow or projectile penetrates only about two inches, and the lungs are spared. Thus, you end up with a muscular and skeletal wound.

When an arrow lodges into the joint or scapula, the deer will usually carry it off. Most often, it breaks off within a short distance. You might find blood on the arrow shaft, but oftentimes it is only at the break of the arrow. If the arrow penetrated further, perhaps up to five inches, the hunter may end up tracking a deer with a wound only to one lung. The chances of a recovery are still not good (see Chapter 7).

It's rare to find blood or hair at the shot location, unless you break bone in the shoulder and the deer drops. Shoulder hair is sometimes found on the shaft of an arrow after it breaks off. The hair will be dark brown or gray with dark tips, and two to two and a half inches long.

You probably won't find blood on the ground until the deer has run thirty to forty yards. The blood trail of a shoulder-shot deer may get better after the deer travels about fifty yards, but this usually brings about false hope. You might also find blood in the deer's tracks. The blood trail will usually subside and stop completely after the deer has traveled 100 to 150 yards. A deer with a shoulder wound probably won't bed down if you do not hit one lung.

High back hits and shoulder wounds seldom prove fatal. However, penetration of an arrow, or trauma caused by a bullet, will increase the tracker's chance of recovering the deer.

Hunters should also be concerned with the "black hole." The black hole is an open area of nothing but muscle, located high on the deer, forward of the scapula close to where the neck joins the shoulder.

When an arrow hits the black hole, it penetrates much better than it does if it hits the scapula. In fact, total penetration is possible. Of course, even a projectile could pass through the black hole. When either an arrow or bullet penetrates the black hole, it passes above the lungs. The wound will probably not result in a downed deer. There may be more external blood loss, but the trail will likely expire after the deer has run 150 to 200 yards. I have tracked numerous whitetails that were hit in the shoulder, but have never recovered any that did not receive a lung wound as well. However, the good news is that most shoulder wounds are superficial. Barring an unlikely infection, the deer should recover.

Conclusion

I sincerely believe that an arrow wound causes much more hemorrhage than a bullet wound, particularly when you deal with the muscle hits discussed in this chapter. Thus, a bowhunter will probably see a better blood trail than the gun hunter who tracks a deer with an identical muscle wound will. However, we know that a bullet wound will cause more trauma and shock than an arrow wound. With these facts in mind, bowhunters should be concerned with blood loss when following the trail. Gun hunters should be concerned with a second shot moments after an animal is hit, since this may be when trauma and shock peaks.

Skeletal wounds should never be taken for granted by anyone. As discussed previously, many deer may drop to the ground after the shot, only to jump up and run away. For this reason, always be prepared to shoot again, even if it appears the deer is down for the count.

Muscle wounds result in the tracker finding bright-red or crimson blood. It's also a fact that some types of muscle wounds bleed better after the deer has traveled 100 yards from the shot location.

It is not always the blood trail that leads a hunter to a downed deer. Many times, it depends upon the hunter's determination, and not giving up unless you know the wound was only superficial.

Chapter 11

Last-Ditch Recovery Tactics

If a deer is not hit in the vitals, there's much more to tracking than following a blood trail. In fact, the blood trail is only the beginning. It will lead you so far, but the rest of the recovery depends upon your knowledge and understanding of the wounded deer, and your determination and effort to locate the animal.

Actually, if a blood trail does not lead you to the deer, it serves one purpose: When it expires, you have at least learned the directional travel of the deer. After that, you can plan an extensive search. I can't begin to tell you how many deer I have recovered, long after the blood trail ended. I have found some deer only a short distance beyond the last drop of blood, while other deer have traveled far from the last blood.

Begin looking for a downed deer only when you are certain a blood trail no longer exists. Then plan an extensive search; don't give up until you have done everything possible to locate the deer. (Photo by Vikki L. Trout.)

Lost Blood Trails

The first thing every hunter should realize is that external bleeding has little to do with whether a deer will go down. Internal hemorrhaging, shock, and trauma kill more deer than external bleeding. If you have faith in this fact, you will put much more effort into locating a deer. Only when you are sure the deer will not go down, and after you have looked thoroughly for the deer, should you give up the trail.

If you have lost the blood trail, follow all deer trails in the area for at least 100 yards, searching for blood and fresh tracks.

Before going on, let me say a couple of things about blood trails. Consider an easy-to-follow blood trail that suddenly stops. It could be that the trail still exists, but the deer changed directions. If a profound blood trail stops, go back to the last drop and begin looking to both sides for more blood. If that doesn't turn up more blood, make sure the deer didn't go back the way it came. If you still find nothing, get closer to the ground. This will help you to see pin-sized drops of blood that you might have missed when you were standing upright.

The time to give up looking for blood and start searching for a downed deer begins after these three things have occurred. 1) All attempts to find more blood on the ground have failed; 2) You cannot find blood that has wiped off on tall weeds and debris; and 3) You cannot locate and follow tracks, scuff marks, or disturbed leaves.

When you begin looking for a downed deer, start where you found the last drop of blood. I can't tell you how many times I have heard hunters tell stories about deer they shot and lost, but found days later only fifty yards from where they stopped tracking.

If an easy-to-follow blood trail suddenly stops, always check to see if the deer made a turn or doubled back. A wounded deer that has traveled a considerable distance will often change direction at the spur of the moment.

Extending the Search

A downed deer is not always easy to see, which is why hunters can walk right by one without noticing it. Tall weeds, brushpiles, and thickets can easily hide a downed deer. For this reason, you must scan the area thoroughly. For instance, if the blood trail headed north, you will usually walk in that direction looking for the deer. However, after walking to the north for a considerable distance, perhaps 100 to 200 yards, you should walk back in the direction you came from. You'll be surprised how you might see a downed deer on the next pass, particularly if the deer's brown back was facing toward you when you walked through the area the first time. When you walk back to where you started, though, the white belly of the deer could be facing toward you. Many downed deer are spotted only because the hunter saw something white.

After losing a blood trail, look into dense areas for the body of the downed deer. This hunter is searching a nearby standing cornfield for the deer.

In a previous chapter, I talked about the number of individuals that should track a deer. Two or three is usually best. However, when it comes to looking for a downed deer, you will want even more eyes searching. Several hunters can cover more ground sooner than one or two can, and you can do it more effectively. But there is a flip side to that theory. I have found that the best person to look for a downed deer is the shooter. His persistence will keep everyone else out there longer, and walking out of their way to search every little crack and cranny for the deer.

When it becomes necessary to widen your search for a downed deer, consider using the zigzag pattern. This is particularly helpful if you must track the deer alone. You begin at the last drop of blood. If the deer was headed north, you walk to the east about fifty yards, then go back to the last blood and walk to the west for fifty yards. As you move farther ahead of the last blood droplet, you should widen your walk to the east and west in fifty-yard increments. If the deer happened to be moving slightly to the west, or to the east when the blood was lost, consider increasing the yardage increments in that direction.

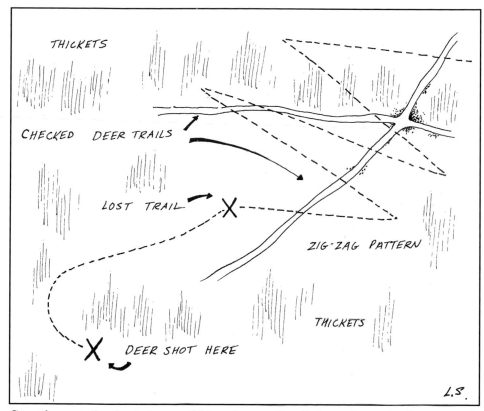

Starting at the last drop of blood, use the "zigzag" method to search for a downed deer. Widen the search as you get further from the last blood.

Anytime you come across a deer trail, walk it for a considerable distance and look for blood and fresh tracks. Wounded deer, primarily those that are walking and not running for their lives, will often walk game trails. If the deer was bleeding on its left side when the blood trail expired, I will look to the left side of the trail for blood, but keep my eyes looking to the center of the trail for blood and tracks. I can't tell you how many times I have followed fresh tracks, only to discover just one more drop of blood down the trail. Normally, I will walk a trail for at least 100 yards to look for more blood and tracks.

You should also search along the banks of ditches and creeks for deer crossings. Even a wounded deer will usually cross these obstacles at an ideal location.

Even better, fresh tracks are usually easy to see along ditches and creeks. If you find fresh tracks, look for blood on each bank. If you don't find blood, follow the trail that crosses the ditch or creek for a long distance, and continue searching for blood. After a wounded deer crosses a steep bank, its heart rate will increase and may cause it to bleed externally.

If the deer was headed toward a road, don't hesitate to walk the road and look for crossing trails. Each time you locate a trail along the road, follow the trail for 100 yards and look for more blood that could put you back on track.

If a deer was headed toward a road, the tracker should walk the road and look for fresh tracks and deer crossings. If he finds any, he should then search for blood. (Photo by Vikki L. Trout.)

Bedding Preferences

If you know places where deer will go to bed down after being wounded, you can increase your chances of finding them by searching these areas thoroughly. Ideal locations include logjams, briars, dense pine thickets, standing cornfields, and honeysuckle. All deer like it thick, but a wounded deer is always anxious to lie in the thickest cover it can find. However, no deer wants to limit its chances of escape. When it walks into thick cover, it will often bed down immediately. For instance, it will not fight its way through 100 yards of dense briars or cutover timber to lie down. Instead, it will accept the first available cover, bed down, and watch its backtrail. Of course, if it can maneuver into additional thick cover without hassle, it may penetrate deeper into the thickets before bedding.

Several years ago, Woody Williams shot an eight-point buck one morning near a pine thicket. His arrow passed through the intestines and the deer loped off. After waiting several hours, we began tracking the deer. By the end of the day, we had covered about 400 yards and had lost the blood trail. As we widened our search to look for a downed deer, I heard something ahead of me. Then I spotted antlers and a slow-moving deer coming out of a honeysuckle thicket. I marked the spot and returned to the other members in the tracking party. After evaluating the situation, and realizing this deer was probably the same buck Woody had shot, we gave up the tracking endeavor until the next day.

The following morning, we looked for blood but could find nothing. Since the deer had entered a forty-acre area of thickets, primarily dense patches of honeysuckle, we decided it best to search every honeysuckle patch thoroughly. Woody's persistence paid off. A couple of hours later, we heard him hollering, "Here he is."

The buck had moved about 150 yards from where I had jumped him the evening before. It passed by several honeysuckle patches before it finally chose one to bed in. The thick patch where the deer laid covered a fifteen-yard circle of terrain. Thankfully, Woody was determined to find this deer. Moreover, he probably would have walked right past the deer had he not penetrated into the precise honeysuckle patch where the deer bedded.

Final Recovery Efforts

I would also suggest you look near water for a downed deer. This is a last resort, but one that shouldn't be overlooked. Few wounded deer go to water, but a few exceptions are enough to make your effort of searching waterholes worthwhile. Dehydration can occur, particularly when it comes to deer hit in the abdomen. As discussed previously, some abdomen-shot deer have bedded down by water after drinking.

Since many scavenging birds are attracted to downed deer, always listen for crows, jays, and ravens. If magpies are common in the area, watch for these scavenging birds as well. A deer does not have to be dead for days to attract scavenging birds. In fact, a downed deer can attract scavengers almost immediately.

A downed deer can attract other types of predators and scavengers, particularly if you are forced to abandon a blood trail overnight These animals either scent the downed deer, or follow its trail. I found one wounded buck after I spotted a coyote leaving a small woodlot. I had shot the deer the evening before and had let the deer go until morning. As I approached the location at dawn the next day, I saw the coyote. Shortly thereafter, I picked up the blood trail and followed it to the downed deer. Sure enough, the coyote, and perhaps another scavenger, had already enjoyed a portion of the deer's hams.

If you will be searching for a downed deer in an unfamiliar area, consider packing along a topographic or aerial map. Knowing the terrain is vitally important. You can mark the spot where you shot the deer, as well as the location where you last found blood. This gives you a precise travel direction, something that will help you if the deer travels a long distance. You can also mark off areas you have already searched, then return to areas you have not searched.

Topo and aerial maps are essential when looking for a downed deer in unfamiliar territory.

If there is a high ridge near the location where you lost the blood trail, search it thoroughly. Many wounded deer will go to high ground to bed down. However, if the deer is aware of the tracking party, it might pull any trick in the book, including going into a marsh. I don't believe a deer is capable of thinking and reasoning. Nonetheless, I do believe their survival instincts are sharp enough to enable them to do unusual things.

If all efforts to locate the deer have failed, ask yourself one question before you stop looking. Have you checked every possible surrounding area for the deer? If you have doubts, make another search. You will feel better about it in the end, even if you don't find the deer. It's much more satisfying to know you did everything possible to recover the animal.

While hunting on Montana rangeland one evening a few years ago, I shot an antelope buck with my bow. The arrow passed through the intestines, and the blood trail was sparse. I tracked the buck for three hours the next morning, and spent another four hours searching the area, hoping to see the downed animal. Disheartened, I gave up the trail and headed for town to prepare for the trip home to Indiana. However, while gassing up the vehicle, I realized that I had not checked a sage coulee on the backend of the ranch. So, Vikki and I headed back to the rangeland and walked almost one mile to reach the coulee. We found that buck within ten minutes.

You can attribute that recovery effort to Lady Luck, Murphy's Law, or just plain old determination. Here's how I see it: If there is one area you don't check, that's where a deer could be down. Had I left for home and not checked the area, it would have eaten at me for days. Even if I had not found the buck in that coulee, I would have been satisfied just to know I had at least looked.

Avoid Assumptions

Finally, don't let speculation distract the facts. When you are looking for a downed deer, it's easy to make assumptions. For instance, you might assume a deer will want to travel in just one particular direction; you could assume that a deer is not hurt badly just because you can't find blood; you could believe that a deer won't go up a steep hill, cross an open field, or traverse a primary road. These assumptions and others will only get you into trouble. In fact, there is only one assumption that the tracker should make: Always assume a wounded deer will do the unexpected. It may not, but thinking that it could will help you to put a superior effort into your recovery tactics.

After the Recovery

Always approach a downed deer cautiously from its backside, studying it carefully all the while. Save the whooping and hollering until you are certain the deer is dead. A deer lying on its side will probably be dead, but not always. You should study a motionless deer thoroughly, regardless of its posture, before you get within touching distance. Try poking the deer with your bow, gun, or a stick to see if there is any reflex. I will also study the deer's eyes. Soon after death, the eyes will appear glazed and look as though a film is covering them. If the deer is still alive, place a shot behind the shoulder of the animal. Using a knife to finish off a deer by cutting its throat is very dangerous. I have done this on a couple of occasions, but only when I believed the deer was close to succumbing. The hooves of a deer are razor sharp and should not be taken lightly. For this reason, if you do not have a gun or bow, back up slowly and find a suitable location where you can watch the deer. If it gets up and moves away, mark the location before you move. Return later with your gun or bow, or consider tracking the animals slowly if the wound calls for immediate pursuit.

If you do recover a deer that was difficult to find, make it a point to examine it carefully when you begin field dressing. Looking at a hole in the deer tells a lot, but not all of the facts. If you cut the animal open very carefully and examine its organs, internal bleeding, and muscle and tissue damage, you'll be surprised how much you can learn about a particular wound. I believe we still have much more to learn about wounded deer.

Throughout this book, I have provided the facts about wounded deer. I did not leave out the suffering. In fact, you could say I took the "blood and gut"

approach to this topic. However, any hunter who is aware of the cold facts is sure
to be a better tracker, and to put a dedicated ethical search into looking for a wounded deer. I'm like you when it comes to shooting a deer. I hope my arrow or projectile passes through the boiler room. The deer dies in seconds and my hunt ends
enjoyably with no suffering to the animal. When the unfortunate happens, though,
you will appreciate all you have learned about the wounded deer.

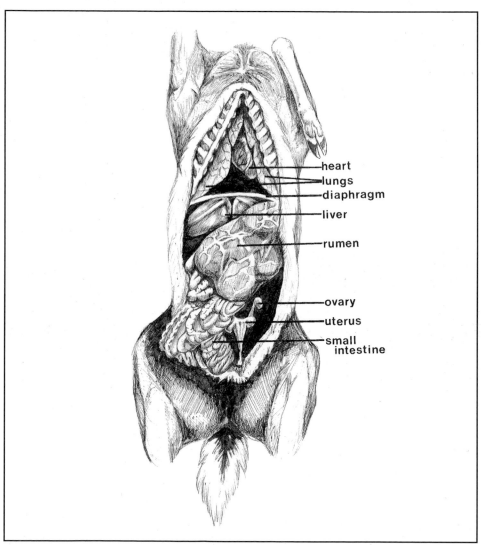

**Internal anatomy of a female white-tailed deer. When field dressing
the deer, look for tissue and organ damage that put the deer down.
(Illustration by Michael Stickney. Courtesy of Wildlife Management
Institute.)**

© Ted Rose

Because of stomach tissue that clogged the exit hole of the arrow, little blood was found. However, persistent tracking led the author to this 11-point buck. Photo by Vikki L. Trout.

Chapter 12

Real-Life Tracking Events

I have provided many anecdotes throughout this book. In my opinion, hearing stories similar to your own experiences is one of the best ways to learn. Although every tracking endeavor differs, it's common for deer with comparable wounds to react in similar manners.

This chapter contains examples of hard-to-recover white-tailed deer, shot with bow and gun. There's little sense in discussing deer with wounds that resulted in quick deaths and easy recoveries in this chapter, since they would not play roles in difficult tracking situations. Many of these anecdotes are accompanied with illustrations, to give you an idea of the deer's travel route. It's worth noting that not all of these cases ended in recoveries.

No. 1: Liver Wound

Two days remained in the archery season as I climbed into my tree stand on the morning of November 11, 1997. The rut was in high gear, and several deer were visiting the acorn trees surrounding my stand.

Two hours into the hunt, I spotted a super eleven-point buck coming toward the oaks. He probably had hopes of picking up the trail of a doe that had visited the acorns earlier. When the deer passed by at twenty-three yards, I released my arrow. Although it quickly vanished through the deer's left side, I knew beyond a doubt that it had hit the buck in the center of his abdomen.

The buck lunged ahead and ran gently for forty yards, then slowed and began walking. He stepped into a thicket some eighty yards away and stood with his head low to the ground. Moments later, he delicately dropped to the ground and bedded.

As I watched the buck, I silently prayed that my arrow had hit the liver. The worst possible scenario would be a stomach wound. However, I felt confident that if nothing went wrong, I would recover the buck. Thirty minutes later, something did go wrong.

I spotted a big ten-point buck, just as big as the one I had shot, slowly approaching the wounded deer. The ears of the newcomer were slicked back, and he appeared ready for battle. When the other buck approached to within a few feet, the wounded buck got up and loped away. When I left the tree stand, it was 9:30 am, about one hour after I had shot the buck.

I returned four hours later with three friends, found my arrow, and examined it closely. The blood was somewhat dark, indicating a possible liver hit. Next, we headed for the buck's bed, where we found very little blood and some hair. We could find no blood when we walked the direction the deer had traveled after leaving the bed.

The other trackers left about 3:00 p.m. and wished me luck. With no blood to follow, I began making a search for the deer, checking every thicket in the surrounding area. One hour later, as I approached a stand of thick saplings about 150 yards from where the buck had bedded that morning, I heard a disturbance. Then I saw him, running out of the thicket. I could see a bloody spot on his abdomen, and had no doubts it was the deer I had shot. The buck had let me get within fifteen yards of him, and probably would have stayed in his bed had I not entered the thicket. In fact, I had passed within forty yards of the thicket earlier that day when searching for blood. I marked the buck's bed and vowed to return the following morning.

I arrived at dawn the next morning with two others, and walked to the bed where I had flushed the buck out of hiding. Again, we found no blood, and we again started an extensive search. I knew the buck would be down, regardless of whether the wound was to his liver, stomach, or both. It took only one hour for me to spot the buck laying in a thick crevice, in a bedded posture that allowed him to see his backtrail. He had traveled 150 yards from where I had jumped him the previous afternoon.

Excitedly, I hollered for the other two trackers to come join me. After congratulations over finding the big buck, I began the task of field dressing the deer, fully expecting to see only a wound to the stomach. However, I quickly discovered that the broadhead had passed through the stomach, and one lobe of the liver. To this day, and after tracking dozens of liver-shot deer, I had never seen one survive for so many hours. He had survived that liver wound for more than eight hours! The buck carried an eleven-point rack, and had a Pope and Young gross score of 141 2/8 inches. He field dressed at 187 pounds.

Although I was in awe after recovering the buck, I had an unbelievable experience the next day, which was the first morning of the firearm season. While sitting in the same tree stand, I shot the ten-point buck that had run off the liver-shot deer two mornings before. This buck had a Boone and Crockett gross score of 141 inches!

No. 2: Stomach Wound

Late in the morning on the first day of the firearm season, my son John saw a buck coming toward his tree stand. Quickly zeroing in on the buck, John squeezed the trigger, and the deer bolted. Although John was pretty sure he had hit the deer, it vanished into thickets and did not provide another shooting opportunity. A minute later, he spotted the buck standing on a nearby hill. Its head was slumped over, and he appeared wounded. The deer then turned and walked off the backside of the hill, out of view.

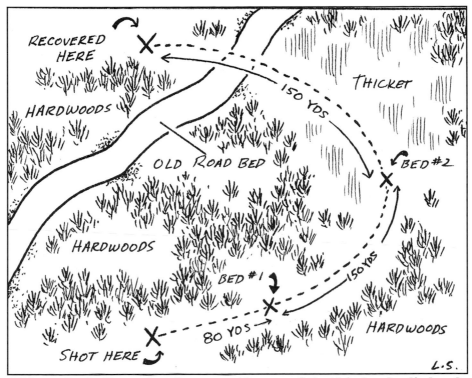

RECOVERED HERE

THICKET

HARDWOODS

150 YDS

OLD ROAD BED

BED #2

HARDWOODS

BED #1

150 YDS

SHOT HERE

80 YDS

HARDWOODS

L.S.

This trail of a liver-shot deer provides proof that big bucks die hard. Unlike most deer with liver wounds that die in less than two hours, this buck survived at least eight hours.

After waiting about thirty minutes, John climbed down and began looking for blood. It didn't take long for him to find it, but the dark blood he found indicated an abdomen wound, and that he should delay tracking the deer.

My wife, Vikki, and I returned with John to the shot location about 2:00 p.m. We picked up John's marker and looked over the blood trail. The deer was walking, and the dark blood droplets were spaced a few feet apart. A short time later, we followed the deer's trail up the hill to where he had stood. As we proceeded to track the deer down the hill, the blood trail became more difficult to follow. The dried blood droplets were smaller, and spaced several feet apart.

During the next couple of hours, we tracked the deer only about 200 yards. We assumed the bullet had hit the stomach or intestines, and hoped the deer would go down before dark. The blood was still dry, and the buck had never bedded.

We eventually lost the blood trail for about thirty minutes. As our search intensified and each tracker got farther apart, however, I finally found more blood. This time, the blood was wet. We quickly regrouped and planned our next strategy. It appeared the buck had bedded somewhere nearby, and we had missed finding the bed. The wet blood also indicated we were close to the deer and had pushed him.

As darkness approached, we placed John in front of me so he could shoot if necessary. Meanwhile I stayed on his tail and continued to find just enough blood to follow the deer. Vikki served as a marker and stayed on the last blood, moving ahead once I found another droplet.

After tracking the wounded buck for ten minutes, with the sun now setting, we heard a disturbance up ahead. John motioned for me to stop as he inched ahead. In front of us, I could see a swamp and an area of cattails. Then I heard the unmistakable sounds of a deer crashing through the cattails. John shouldered his gun and fired. It had finally ended.

Although the buck had survived for many hours, John claimed the deer was about to go down for keeps. He had allowed John to get within twenty yards, and he was stumbling when he fled. Upon examining the buck, we found the projectile had passed through only the deer's stomach.

No. 3: Brisket and Front Leg Wound

It was the late archery season when the buck entered the thicket just before dusk. He approached within twenty-five yards of my wife's tree stand and stood quartering away. Vikki took careful aim and released the arrow. As the arrow hit, she heard both a dull thump and loud crack. The buck lunged forward and ran hard, quickly vanishing in the darkening woods.

When Vikki called me on the two-way radio a few minutes later, I advised her to leave the stand quietly and meet me out on the road to discuss the details. She could not find her arrow, nor had she found any blood or hair at the shot location.

After my son met us on the road, the three of us headed into the dark woods in an attempt to determine if she had hit the deer. We knew the dull thump could have been the arrow hitting the deer, but the loud crack she heard could have been bone, or even a tree if she had missed the buck. However, after a few minutes of searching the area, I found bright-red blood only ten yards from the shot location. The bright blood signaled us to pursue the deer immediately.

Although she shot at the deerís left side, the blood was on the right side of the deer's trail, close to his tracks. After following the blood trail for thirty yards, we found her arrow. The entire shaft was drenched in bright-red blood and bent about six inches below the nock.

The blood trail intensified as we continued following the deer. However, after 125 yards, we had doubts the arrow had penetrated the chest cavity. To confirm our theory, we soon began finding blood in the deer's right track, and in the center of the trail. We also found a few drops near the left side of the trail, and determined the deer was walking. It appeared the arrow had caught the left side of the brisket and the right leg, due to the deer quartering away.

During the next two hours, we followed the blood trail into a strip-mined area. The deer seemed to be maneuvering up and down the small hills with little trouble, although we did find occasional scuffmarks. The buck soon left the strip mines and entered some hardwoods. The blood trail began to diminish and it appeared as if coagulation had begun. Just after we lost the trail, I heard sounds of a deer moving up ahead. With this in mind, and no blood to follow, we called off the tracking until morning.

Vikki and I returned just after dawn and found our marker that designated the last drop of blood. We soon found dried blood and picked up the trail. Although there was less blood than what we found the previous night, we could still follow the buck's trail.

Although at times the blood became difficult to follow, we were able to stay on the trail for the next four hours. But then things got worse. We could find only one drop of blood about every ten yards, and the tracking became slow and tedious. At 1:00 p.m., we called off the search and headed home.

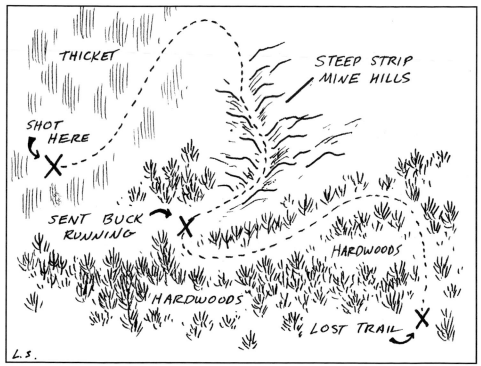

A deer with a leg wound can often be tracked for a long distance. Trackers followed the trail of this deer for 1.5 miles before losing the blood trail for good.

We spent ten hours tracking and searching for the buck, which had covered about one and a half miles. We did not find any bone fragments along the trail. The buck never bedded. Just before we lost the blood trail for good, we could see that most of the blood droplets came from the right leg and the center of the trail, as they did previously. I must believe the arrow passed through the forward portion of the brisket on the deer's left side, and into the buck's right front leg. The arrow had missed the heart. Tallow from the brisket would not have been obvious on the arrow shaft after it passed through the leg. The bend in the arrow also indicates that the buck's left front leg hit against the nock end of the arrow when the deer ran off with the shaft sticking through the right front leg.

No. 4: Heart and Leg Hit

After an unproductive morning bowhunt, I pulled my vehicle to the side of the road and talked with my good friend Woody Williams. Minutes later, his son Mark showed up and presented a bloody arrow. We examined it closely. The blood appeared crimson red, and we found stiff hair on the shaft. Mark explained the reactions of the deer he had shot. He said the arrow seemed to fly a little low. Upon being hit, the buck jumped and ran away hard, but soon slowed and began walking. The deer also seemed to have problems maneuvering, indicating a possible leg wound.

Since there was no dark blood, we decided to pursue the wounded deer immediately. About an hour had passed since Mark had shot the buck, and we knew it was probably best to get on the deer's trail before coagulation became a problem.

After picking up the blood trail and quietly following it about fifty yards, we determined the deer was indeed walking. Each blood droplet was spaced about one foot apart, and we could easily see the dried blood. However, we soon began finding bright-red blood on the right side of the deer's trail, and crimson-red blood on the left side. It was then that we had to consider a brisket and leg wound.

We had followed the trail another fifty yards when I heard the deer crashing through brush up ahead. However, it sounded more like a deer falling to the ground than a deer running away. We inched forward a few more yards, then spotted the buck down in a thicket, still alive. Mark walked ahead of Woody and I, and disposed of the deer with a clean shot to the lungs.

Mark's first arrow had passed through the buck's brisket and sliced the heart. After exiting the brisket, it struck the upper part of the right front leg, which resulted in the bright-red blood.

Many hunters have discovered that some heart-shot deer, particularly those with nicks to the heart, do not go down within seconds. Mark's deer had lived for ninety minutes and traveled about 150 yards.

No. 5: Intestinal Wound

It had been a productive morning bowhunt during the pre-rut period in Illinois. From my tree stand, I watched two eight-point bucks attempting to settle a dispute over a doe. However, since neither buck offered a shooting opportunity, I was grateful to see the nine-point buck that approached to within thirty yards later in the morning. When the deer stood broadside, I settled my sights just behind his shoulder and released the arrow. As sometimes happens, the arrow hit brush and deflected, hitting the buck low and just in front of the hips.

After the shot, the deer loped off and stopped a short distance away. He stood there for several minutes with his head low to the ground. Then, the hunkered buck walked slowly out of sight, with his legs widespread.

I waited thirty minutes, then climbed down quietly and retrieved my arrow. It had only a couple of specks of blood about halfway down the shaft, and a few white hairs near the broadhead. There was little odor to the arrow, although I could see dark brown contents from the intestines. After finding no blood near the shot location, I walked a few yards to where the buck had stood for so long. There, I found a few small drops of blood. I determined that the arrow had entered the deer about three inches up from his bottom, and exited around his penis. I then snuck out of the area.

I returned to where the deer had stood at about 2:00 p.m. My nephew, Todd Litsey, and Vikki assisted. It had been seven hours since I had shot the buck, and I knew that we were in for a difficult tracking.

Tediously, we followed the blood trail about 150 yards through thickets. By this time, the dime-sized blood droplets had decreased to pin-sized droplets. The blood trail then diminished completely. Up until dark, we searched for blood and beds, but found nothing.

At dawn the following morning, the three of us began an extensive search for the buck. We assumed he would be down, but knew it could take hours to find him in the half-mile stretch of thickets that lay ahead.

It was around 9:00 a.m., about 400 yards from where we had last found blood the previous afternoon, that Todd spotted the deer getting out of a bed about sixty yards ahead in the hardwoods. He said the buck moved very slowly, like an old man getting out of a chair. He watched the buck as it moved away and into a honeysuckle thicket along the edge of a plowed field.

We decided the buck would probably lie down again if we left him alone. And since I did not have my bow along, we thought it best to sneak out of the area, have lunch, and return. I hoped that postponing the tracking endeavor would keep the buck in the nearby thickets. If all went well, he would be dead by the time we returned.

Four hours of daylight remained when we walked into the woods where we last saw the buck. Our game plan was to have Todd and Vikki walk into the honeysuckle thicket from the north. With me on the south side of the thicket in the narrow wooded funnel, we figured the buck would come my way if it were still alive. I had my bow, and would attempt to shoot the deer again if he passed by. However, the buck did not emerge from the thicket when Todd and Vikki passed along the edge of the honeysuckle. The three of us then got together, approached the thicket, and looked it over carefully. No buck. I did find a bloody bed, and assumed the buck was still nearby.

After debating the situation, we decided Todd and Vikki should walk to the upper end of the wooded corridor. There were many more thickets, and the possibility existed that they would push the deer to me. However, that plan also backfired. When they approached, they shook their heads in dismay. They had walked through the thickets in the narrow corridor, and had seen no sign of the buck. Tired and distressed, with darkness getting closer, I called off the tracking event.

I came back the next morning with Vikki. We spent several hours scanning the dense honeysuckle for the buck. We also checked the area where the blood trail originated, just in case the buck had doubled back. Then I searched the plowed field, and although I found dozens of fresh deer tracks, I could not find blood. The field was 400 yards wide, and the deer would have had to cross the entire width of the field to reach woods on the other side. This seemed unlikely, but he might have walked the open field since he knew we were in pursuit. So, we headed across the field and searched the thickets in one last attempt to locate the buck. After finding nothing, I gave up the search late in the afternoon.

A few days later, while I was away on a hunting trip, Todd heard that the landowner had seen the buck walk slowly across the plowed field the day we jumped him. Eager to know if the buck was there, Todd returned to the area and walked across the field to make a thorough search of the thickets. He found the buck about 100 yards into the thickets next to a pond. Vikki and I had missed seeing the buck by about fifty yards.

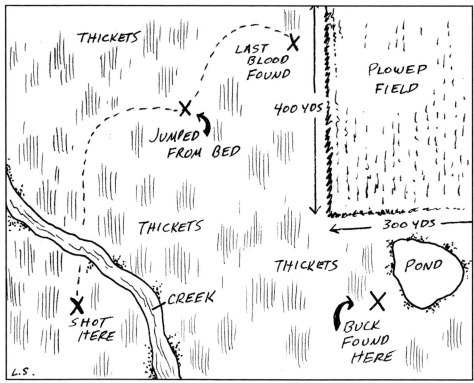

The author and other trackers spent several hours over a period of three days searching for this intestinal-shot Illinois buck.

No. 6: Liver and One Lung Shot

Dean Stallion, a taxidermist and avid hunter, headed for the woods with his blackpowder gun on the first day of Indiana's 1991 muzzleloader season. That morning, an eleven-point buck attempted to walk past his stand sixty yards away. Just before the deer got out of view, it turned and quartered slightly toward Dean. Stallion put his sights on the front shoulder and squeezed the trigger. The deer ran away hard, and was visible only for about thirty yards.

A short time later, Dean climbed down and walked to the shot location. He immediately found dark blood and suspected a liver or stomach shot. He cautiously backed off and opted to wait a few hours before tracking the buck.

Dean returned with a friend about three hours later and picked up the trail of dark blood. The trail was easy to follow for more than 300 yards. Interestingly, after tracking the deer for a short distance, the pair began finding bright-red blood along the trail. Some of the bright blood contained air bubbles.

As Dean began to follow the blood up a small hill, he spotted the buck lying above him about seventy-five yards away, watching him. Unfortunately, the buck got up and vanished over the back of the hill before Dean could shoulder his gun.

The two trackers then discussed the pursuit and decided what to do next. The bright blood had confused them, and they were now unsure if it was best to pursue the deer immediately, or wait. They even wondered if the deer had a wound to one lung. They decided it best to continue tracking the deer.

During the next hour, Dean said he heard the deer moving ahead of him at least three times. The buck would apparently stand in one location until the trackers got so close, then move away. Dean had hoped to get another shot, but the opportunity never presented itself. Finally, after the deer went into an open area, the blood trail was lost and the tracking was temporarily called off.

Knowing that the dark blood indicated a shot to the abdomen, and that the deer should soon go down, Dean called me to help him locate the deer. Two hours of daylight remained when we got to the location where he had lost the blood trail.

We searched frantically over a wide area and found no blood, or beds with blood in them. Just before dark, we decided to check another area that we had not previously walked through. Just as I came around the corner of a hill, I picked up the scent of a buck. As sometimes happens, you can smell a rutting buck. Sure enough, there was Dean's buck, only fifty yards away.

The buck had died in a bedded posture, watching his backtrail. It had been dead for awhile, and some stiffness was apparent. Upon field dressing the deer, Dean determined the projectile had hit one lung and the liver.

No. 7: One Lung Shot

Typically, only a handful of hunters go afield during the late archery season. Indiana bowhunter Tim Hillsmeyer is one of those die-hard hunters who will always hunt to the end if he hasn't filled his tag during the early season.

One evening just before Christmas, after a light snow, Tim saw eleven antlerless deer moving toward a wheat field. Then he spotted a monster eight-pointer. The big deer passed under Tim's stand, but did not offer a shooting opportunity. When the buck was twenty-three yards away, however, it turned slightly and quartered away. Tim released the arrow and watched with enthusiasm. However, the arrow appeared to go along the ribs and fail to penetrate effectively. Meanwhile, the deer ran away hard. Tim watched the deer go across a field for about 125 yards before it disappeared.

With the light fading, Tim climbed down and picked up the tracks of the deer in the snow. He followed the tracks for the distance he had watched the deer, but found no blood.

Tim left the area and met with his brother, only to return a short time later with flashlights. The two walked to where Tim had last found tracks in the snow. At first, they could find nothing. However, after an intense search, they located two small specks of blood. They attempted to follow the buck by its tracks, but he soon entered a pine thicket where there was no snow. It now appeared that better lights and more eyes were necessary. Tim returned home, picked up his son Justin, and a lantern.

Shortly after the trackers went into the pine thicket, Tim found the back half of his arrow. The arrow lay on the ground about 200 yards from the shot location. A short distance ahead of the arrow, Tim found a bed that contained a small amount of blood. The blood trail that left the bed was sparse, but visible enough to follow. Eventually, the trackers lost the trail when it hit an old roadbed. At 10:30 p.m., they called off the search and decided to wait for morning.

At dawn, Tim and Justin were greeted with an inch of new snow. Tim knew that the snow had covered the blood and tracks that were there the night before. With this in mind, he and his son spread out and began searching for the buck. As Tim headed for a nearby grown-up field to look for the deer, Justin hollered, "I see a buck!" Tim quickly asked if it was dead or alive, and Justin confirmed that it was a downed deer.

As Tim field dressed the deer, he found the business end of the arrow in the deer. It had deflected upwards, probably when it hit a rib bone. The entry hole was on the deer's left side, and the broadhead had come only a quarter inch out, on the right shoulder. The body cavity was also filled with blood. Tim claims the buck was quite warm, and had probably lived for most of the cold night. The one-lung shot deer had traveled about 500 yards.

No. 8: Ham Shot

When I took the quartering-away shot, the arrow hit a little too far back and struck the buck in the ham. The shaft seemed to penetrate about six inches. There was no loud crack to indicate a bone hit, and it appeared I was dealing with a severe muscle wound, or a severed femoral artery. However, I remained hopeful, knowing that I usually recover ham-shot deer, even if the femoral artery is spared.

The buck ran hard into a dense thicket after being hit. He was visible for only a few seconds, but I could hear him crashing away for a long distance. When all was quiet, I evaluated the situation. The buck had no problems maneuvering after the shot, and the arrow was plainly visible when the deer ran off. I had no doubts of the wound location, and knew I should get after him quickly.

Indiana bowhunter Tim Hillsmeyer tagged this buck during the late archery season, but only after he and others followed the deer tediously for several hours. The buck covered about 500 yards after being hit in only one lung.

A few minutes had passed by the time I climbed down from my tree stand and got to the shot location. Although I didn't see blood where the buck stood when I shot, I could see droplets ten yards away. I picked up the trail and easily followed it through the thicket. The buck was bleeding profusely, but I remained skeptical. The blood was not splattered several feet from the trail as it sometimes does when you hit the femoral artery. Instead, the blood droplets were only about one foot from the deer's tracks.

After following the trail through the thickets for a short distance, I heard him ahead of me. Then I got a glimpse of him as he left his bed. He was now having problems maneuvering his left leg, and he quickly slowed to a walk. Meanwhile, I had hopes he would not travel far before bedding again. I sat down for a few minutes, but decided it best to continue the pursuit, providing the blood would continue to be easy to follow. It was. Within ten minutes, I had moved 125 yards from the bed where I had jumped the buck. Then I saw him struggling to get out of another bed. I easily approached within bow range and placed an arrow through his lungs.

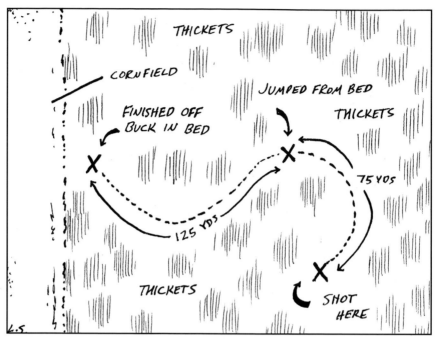

The ham-shot buck bedded twice and traveled a total distance of 200 yards before it was finally shot again.

That ham-shot deer traveled a total distance of 200 yards. Of course, had I not jumped the buck from the bed, it probably wouldn't have traveled that far. Pushing the buck, though, was probably best to prevent coagulation. The muscle wound was severe, as it usually is when an arrow or projectile penetrates the ham.

The author has made notes about several hundred tracking experiences that he has been involved in for more than three decades. These notes have provided valuable insight for future tracking endeavors. Photo by Vikki L. Trout.

Interestingly, the trail of every wounded deer is unique. The color of the blood, the color, texture and length of the hair, and the pattern of the blood trail can provide vivid details about each type of wound.

Chapter 13

Quick Reference Guide

This chapter could become the most important chapter of all if you carry this book into the field. It provides a short-version summary for most types of wounds, and guidelines for you to follow before and during tracking. If you need more details, refer to the chapter that discusses the descriptive science of the wound. However, many of the questions you will ask yourself can be answered here.

A buck any hunter would be proud of. If you have to track him, the following guidelines will help.

None of the tracking suggestions that follow is carved in stone. They are merely guidelines. However, most often, if you follow the methods and suggestions provided in this chapter, you will considerably increase your chances of recovering the animal. Some things provided here are fact. For instance, a stomach-shot deer will leave blood that's much darker than a deer with a muscle wound. Blood colors, though, can vary accordingly when different wounds exist. The animal you track may leave both dark and bright blood, simply because two wounds occurred.

Double-Lung Shot

1. Hair description: Dark brown or gray with black tips, 2.25 to 2.75 inches long.
2. Blood color: Bright red, sometimes pink.
3. Reaction of deer: Usually runs hard with belly low to the ground.
4. Waiting time before tracking: Twenty minutes.
5. Blood-trailing expectations: Easy to follow, increases as you trail (unless deer is hit high), possibly foamy blood.
6. Distance traveled before succumbing or bedding: Drops within 100 to 150 yards, sometimes less.

One-Lung Hit

1. Hair description: Dark brown or gray with black tips, 2.25 to 2.75 inches long.
2. Blood color: Bright red.
3. Reaction of deer: Usually runs hard at first but slows up after 100 yards.
4. Waiting time before tracking: Twenty minutes.
5. Blood-trailing expectations: Blood increases after fifty yards but slows up after 125 yards; you may find some air bubbles in blood.
6. Distance traveled before succumbing or bedding: May bed down within 150 to 200 yards.

Heart Shot

1. Hair description: Dark brown or gray with black tips, 2.25 to 2.75 inches long.
2. Blood color: Crimson red.
3. Reaction of deer: Runs very erratically at first.
4. Waiting time before tracking: Twenty minutes.
5. Blood-trailing expectations: Blood trail is steady up to where deer drops.
6. Distance traveled before succumbing or bedding: 100 yards, but can be further.

Liver Hit

1. Hair description: Dark brown or gray with black tips, two to 2.5 inches long.
2. Blood color: Dark red (similar to maroon), but not as dark as stomach or intestinal blood.
3. Reaction of deer: Lunges and runs hard, but often slows and walks after seventy-five yards.
4. Waiting time before tracking: Two to three hours.
5. Blood-trailing expectations: Enough blood on ground to follow if deer is walking, but usually less blood if a stomach wound also exists.
6. Distance traveled before succumbing or bedding: Usually beds down within 150 yards, but should succumb in less than 250 yards if not pushed.

Stomach Shot

1. Hair description: Dark gray or brown, two to 2.5 inches long, coarse with lighter tips than chest hair. Belly hair is white to gray, coarse, slightly twisted and 2.25 to 2.5 inches long.
2. Blood color: Dark red (darker than liver wound but not as dark as intestinal wound).
3. Reaction of deer: Often jumps, takes a few bounds, and stops. May only flinch and run gently. Body appears hunched, legs widespread.
4. Waiting time before tracking: Four to six hours.
5. Blood-trailing expectations: Usually found within fifty yards of where shot. Holes are often plugged with organ tissue, and very little blood is found. Blood trail may be better if spleen or stomach artery is also severed.
6. Distance traveled before succumbing or bedding: Usually beds down within 150 yards and will not go much farther unless pushed.

Intestinal Wound

1. Hair description: Side hair is coarse, dark brown or gray with lighter tips than chest hair. Belly hair is coarse, 2.5 to 2.75 inches long, and very curly.
2. Blood color: Very dark red, sometimes almost black.
3. Reaction of deer: Hunches up and runs sluggishly. May jump and stand for several seconds or even minutes before walking off.
4. Waiting time before tracking: Eight to 12 hours.
5. Blood-trailing expectations: Usually begins bleeding externally within fifty yards, but holes are often plugged by intestinal tissue. May find no blood at all, or only pin-sized drops.
6. Distance traveled before succumbing or bedding: Usually beds down within 200 yards. However, deer may leave bed and travel much farther before bedding again.

Kidney Shot

1. Hair description: Very coarse, dark brown or gray with black tips, 2.5 to 2.75 inches long.
2. Blood color: Crimson red.
3. Reaction of deer: Jumps up or lunges forwards and goes into hard run, but not as hard as deer hit in lungs. Sometimes walks and begins staggering last few yards.
4. Waiting time before tracking: Twenty minutes.
5. Blood trailing expectations: Blood usually found within fifteen yards. Blood may also spurt to sides of trail.
6. Distance traveled before succumbing or bedding: Succumbs in less than 100 yards.

Femoral Artery Wound

1. Hair description: Very coarse, dark brown or gray with dark tips, two to 2.25 inches long (shorter than chest hair but not as long as lower leg hair).
2. Blood color: Bright red.
3. Reaction of deer: Usually runs hard but may have trouble motivating due to muscle damage.
4. Waiting time before tracking: Twenty minutes.
5. Blood-trailing expectations: Blood found within a few yards. Blood usually spurts to sides of trail.
6. Distance traveled before succumbing or bedding: Succumbs within 100 yards.

Aorta Artery Wound

1. Hair description: Dark brown or gray with black tips, 2.25 to 2.5 inches long, but shorter than hair on top of back.
2. Blood color: Bright red.
3. Reaction of deer: Runs hard and sometimes erratically.
4. Waiting time before tracking: Twenty minutes.
5. Blood-trailing expectations: Blood found within twenty to thirty yards, sometimes spurting to the sides of trail.
6. Distance traveled before succumbing or bedding: Succumbs within 150 yards.

Carotid or Jugular Wound

1. Hair description: Very short (1.5 to 1.75 inches), fine, and light gray. May be white if projectile passes through the underside of neck.
2. Blood color: Bright red.
3. Reaction of deer: Runs hard, but not as hard as a lung-shot deer.
4. Waiting time before tracking: Twenty minutes.
5. Blood-trailing expectations: Blood often found immediately. Blood spurts up to two feet away from trail.
6. Distance traveled before succumbing or bedding: Succumbs within 100 yards.

Spine/Neck Vertebrate Hit

1. Hair description: Spine hair is very long (2.5 to 2.75 inches), very coarse, hollow, dark gray with black tips. Neck hair is very short (1.5 to 1.75 inches), fine, and light gray. May be white if projectile passes through the underside of neck.
2. Blood color: Back blood is crimson red. Neck muscle blood is bright red.
3. Reaction of deer: Drops immediately, but may have some mobility if vertebrate is severed behind the shoulder.
4. Waiting time before tracking: Zero.

5. Blood-trailing expectations: Blood may splatter in different directions where deer drops.
6. Distance traveled before succumbing or bedding: Drops immediately, but may have some mobility.

Ham Shot

1. Hair description: Short length (two inches), very coarse, dark brown or gray with black tips.
2. Blood color: Bright red.
3. Reaction of deer: Runs hard but may have problems with motivation.
4. Waiting time before tracking: Twenty minutes.
5. Blood-trailing expectations: Blood often found at shot location, and usually intensifies as deer travels farther away. Blood is often found in deer's tracks after it travels seventy-five to 100 yards.
6. Distance traveled before succumbing or bedding: Usually beds down within 150 yards of where it was shot. A second shot may be necessary.

Shoulder Shot

1. Hair description: Medium length (two to 2.5 inches), dark brown or gray with dark tips.
2. Blood color: Bright red.
3. Reaction of deer: Runs hard, but may drop to ground temporarily if scapula is broken.
4. Waiting time before tracking: Twenty minutes.
5. Blood-trailing expectations: First blood found after thirty to forty yards, and sometimes appears in the deer's tracks. Blood may intensify after seventy-five yards but will expire completely after 100 to 150 yards.
6. Distance traveled before succumbing or bedding: Seldom beds down.

Loin Wound

1. Hair description: Long (2.25 to 2.50 inches), very coarse, dark gray with black tips.
2. Blood color: Crimson red.
3. Reaction of deer: Often runs as hard as a lung-shot deer, but slows up and walks after 100 yards if not spooked.
4. Waiting time before tracking: Twenty minutes.
5. Blood trailing expectations: First blood shows up after deer travels forty to fifty yards. Will then increase for a short distance before subsiding.
6. Distance traveled before succumbing or bedding: Often beds down after traveling 150 to 200 yards.

Neck Wound

1. Hair description: Very short (1.5 to 1.75 inches), fine, and light gray. May be white if arrow or projectile passes through the underside of neck.
2. Blood color: Bright red.
3. Reaction of deer: Drops if vertebrate is crushed. Usually runs hard if only muscles are severed, but head may be low to the ground.
4. Waiting time before tracking: Twenty minutes.
5. Blood-trailing expectations: Bleeds well externally, and blood may be found near the center of the trail. Blood trail often gets better after the deer has run 100 yards, but will begin to subside after 250 yards.
6. Distance traveled before succumbing or bedding: Sometimes beds down after traveling 150 yards.

Windpipe Hit

1. Hair description: Dark brown or gray with black tips, 1.75 to two inches long (shorter than most body hair).
2. Blood color: Bright red.
3. Reaction of deer: Usually lunges ahead and runs hard.
4. Waiting time before tracking: Twenty minutes.
5. Blood-trailing expectations: Prevailing blood trail, and you may find air bubbles.
6. Distance traveled before succumbing or bedding: May succumb within 150 yards if windpipe is crushed (much less if carotid artery and/or jugular vein is hit).

Brisket Wound

1. Hair description: Dark brown or gray with black tips, 2.50 to 2.75 inches long, stiff and may curl.
2. Blood color: Crimson red (tallow present on arrow).
3. Reaction of deer: May run, but often lunges forward and stands.
4. Waiting time before tracking: Twenty minutes.
5. Blood-trailing expectations: Minimal blood found, trail often subsides after 100 to 150 yards.
6. Distance traveled before succumbing or bedding: Seldom beds down, and will not succumb unless arrow or projectile hits the heart.

Leg Wound

1. Hair description: Very coarse, dark brown or gray, short (1.5 inches), and stiff.
2. Blood color: Bright red.
3. Reaction of deer: Runs clumsily when bone is broken.

4. Waiting time before tracking: Twenty minutes.

5. Blood-trailing expectations: Blood found at shot location, and in the deer's tracks after it begins walking. Blood trail increases the first 100 yards but then tapers.

6. Distance traveled before succumbing or bedding: Usually beds within 150 to 200 yards.